ALL ABOUT COFFEE

A HISTORY OF COFFEE FROM THE CLASSIC TRIBUTE TO THE WORLD'S MOST BELOVED BEVERAGE

WILLIAM H. UKERS

Avon, Massachusetts

Contains material adapted and abridged from *All about Coffee*, by
William H. Ukers, M.A., originally published by The Tea and Coffee
Trade Journal Company, 1922.

Published by
Adams Media, a division of F+W Media, Inc.
57 Littlefield Street, Avon, MA 02322. U.S.A.
www.adamsmedia.com

ISBN 10: 1-4405-5631-8
ISBN 13: 978-1-4405-5631-9
eISBN 10: 1-4405-5632-6
eISBN 13: 978-1-4405-5632-6

Printed in the United States of America.

10   9   8   7   6   5   4   3   2   1

This publication is designed to provide accurate and authoritative
information with regard to the subject matter covered. It is sold with
the understanding that the publisher is not engaged in rendering legal,
accounting, or other professional advice. If legal advice or other expert
assistance is required, the services of a competent professional person
should be sought.

—From a *Declaration of Principles* jointly adopted by a
Committee of the American Bar Association and a Committee
of Publishers and Associations

Many of the designations used by manufacturers and sellers to distinguish
their product are claimed as trademarks. Where those designations
appear in this book and Adams Media was aware of a trademark claim,
the designations have been printed with initial capital letters.

This book is available at quantity discounts for bulk purchases.
For information, please call 1-800-289-0963.

CONTENTS

INTRODUCTION
TO THIS EDITION

William H. Ukers, the founder of the well-respected (and still active) *Tea and Coffee Trade Journal*, set out to write the definitive guide to coffee in 1905.

He spent years traveling around the world, researching the countries where coffee trees were grown and harvested, sorting and classifying the different varieties of beans, and examining the methods of producing what he called the "fighting man's drink." He sought out libraries in Europe with rare historical texts that would shed light on this beloved beverage. He took weeks, even months, to verify each anecdote. He worked with Charles W. Trigg, an industrial fellow of the Mellon Institute of Industrial Research, to examine coffee's medical properties.

The original edition of *All about Coffee* took seventeen years to complete. Finally published in 1922, Ukers's 700-page opus covered the earliest forms of the beverage up until his "modern-day." William H. Ukers gushes over coffee as only the most ardent caffeine addict could—calling it "a psychological necessity" and defending it from attacks from "religious superstition, medical prejudice, fierce political opposition, stupid fiscal restrictions, unjust taxes, and irksome duties."

This edition of *All about Coffee* culls the best and brightest of Ukers's research and observations. The result is a delightful book of tidbits and aphorisms as illuminating and energizing as a morning cup of coffee.

FOREWORD

Civilization, in its onward march, has produced only three important non-alcoholic beverages—the extract of the tea plant, the extract of the cocoa bean, and the extract of the coffee bean.

Leaves and beans—these are the vegetable sources of the world's favorite nonalcoholic table beverages. Of the two, the tea leaves lead in total amount consumed; the coffee beans are second; and the cocoa beans are a distant third, although advancing steadily. But in international commerce, coffee beans occupy a far more important position than either of the others, being imported into nonproducing countries to twice the extent of tea leaves.

Coffee is universal in its appeal. All nations do it homage. It has become recognized as a human necessity. It is no longer a luxury or an indulgence; it is a corollary of human energy and human efficiency. People love coffee because of its two-fold effect—the pleasurable sensation and the increased efficiency it produces.

Coffee has an important place in the rational diet of all the civilized peoples of earth. It is a democratic beverage. Not only is it the drink of fashionable society; it is also a favorite beverage of the men and women who do the world's work, whether they toil with brain or brawn. It has been acclaimed "the most grateful lubricant known to the human machine," and "the most delightful taste in all nature."

No nonalcoholic drink has ever encountered as much opposition as coffee. Given to the world by the church and dignified by the medical profession, it has nevertheless had to suffer from religious superstition and medical prejudice. During the thousand years of its development, it has experienced fierce political opposition, stupid fiscal restrictions, unjust taxes, irksome duties; but, surviving all of these, it has triumphantly moved on to a foremost place in the catalog of popular beverages.

But coffee is something more than a beverage. It is one of the world's greatest adjuvant foods. There are other auxiliary foods, but none that excels it for palatability and comforting effects, the psychology of which is to be found in its unique flavor and aroma.

Men and women drink coffee because it adds to their sense of well-being. It not only smells good and tastes good to all mankind, but all respond to its wonderful stimulating properties. The chief factors in coffee goodness are the caffeine content and the coffee's natural oil, called caffeol. Caffeine increases the capacity for muscular and mental work without harmful reaction. The caffeol supplies the flavor and the aroma —that indescribable exotic fragrance that woos us through the nostrils, forming one of the principal elements that make up the lure of coffee.

Good coffee, carefully roasted and properly brewed, produces a natural beverage that, for tonic effect,

cannot be surpassed, even by its rivals, tea and cocoa. Here is a drink that 97 percent of individuals
find harmless and wholesome, and without which life
would be drab indeed—a pure, safe, and helpful stimulant compounded in nature's own laboratory, and one
of the chief joys of life!

THE
PHILOSOPHY
OF
COFFEE

The Effect of Coffee

Carl V. Voit, the German physiological chemist, says this about coffee:

> The effect of coffee is that we are bothered less by unpleasant experiences and become more able to conquer difficulties; therefore, for the feasting rich, it makes intestinal work after a meal less evident and drives away the deadly ennui; for the student it is a means to keep wide awake and fresh; for the worker it makes the day's fatigue more bearable.

Coffee and the Promotion of Intellectualism

The coffee houses became the gathering places for wits, fashionable people, and brilliant and scholarly men, to whom they afforded opportunity for endless gossip and discussion. It was only natural that the lively interchange of ideas at these public clubs should generate liberal and radical opinions, and that the constituted authorities should look askance at them. Indeed the consumption of coffee has been curiously associated with movements of political protest in its whole history, at least up to the nineteenth century.

Coffee has promoted clear thinking and right living wherever introduced. It has gone hand in hand with the world's onward march toward democracy.

//

Coffee and Revolution

One of the most interesting facts in the history of the coffee drink is that wherever it has been introduced, it has spelled revolution. It has been the world's most radical drink in that its function has always been to make people think. And when the people began to think, they became dangerous to tyrants and to foes of liberty of thought and action. Sometimes the people became intoxicated with their newfound ideas, and, mistaking liberty for license, they ran amuck and called down upon their heads persecutions and many petty intolerances.

The Genius's Drink of Choice

D r. Charles B. Reed, professor in the medical school of Northwestern University, says that coffee may be considered as a type of substance that fosters genius. History seems to bear him out. Coffee's essential qualities are so well defined, says Dr. Reed, that one critic has claimed the ability to trace throughout the works of Voltaire those portions that came from coffee's inspiration. Tea and coffee promote a harmony of the creative faculties that permits the mental concentration necessary to produce the masterpieces of art and literature.

Voltaire and Balzac were the most ardent devotees of coffee among the French literati. Voltaire, the king of wits, was the king of coffee drinkers. Even in his old age, he was said to have consumed fifty cups daily.

To the abstemious Balzac, coffee was both food and drink. In Frederick Lawton's *Balzac* we read: "Balzac worked hard. His habit was to go to bed at six in the evening, sleep till twelve, and, after, to rise and write for nearly twelve hours at a stretch, imbibing coffee as a stimulant through these spells of composition."

In his *Treatise on Modern Stimulants*, Balzac thus describes his reaction to his most beloved stimulant:

This coffee falls into your stomach, and straightway there is a general commotion. Ideas begin to move like the battalions of the Grand Army on the battlefield, and the battle takes place. Things remembered arrive at full gallop, ensign to the wind. The light cavalry of comparisons deliver a magnificent deploying charge, the artillery of logic hurry up with their train and ammunition, the shafts of wit start up like sharpshooters. Similes arise, the paper is covered with ink; for the struggle commences and is concluded with torrents of black water, just as a battle with powder.

In his novel *Ursule Mirouët*, Balzac describes how Doctor Minoret used to regale his friends with a cup of "Moka," mixed with bourbon and Martinique, which the doctor insisted on personally preparing in a silver coffee pot. It is Balzac's own custom that he is detailing. He would only buy his bourbon in the rue Mont Blanc (now the chaussé d'Antin), the Martinique in the rue des Vielles Audriettes, and the "Moka" at a grocer's in the rue de l'Université. It was half a day's journey to fetch them.

Sir James Mackintosh, the Scottish philosopher and statesman, was so fond of coffee that he used to assert that the powers of a man's mind would generally be found to be proportional to the quantity of that stimulant which he drank.

Cowper; Parson and Parr, the famous Greek scholars; Dr. Samuel Johnson; and William Hazlitt were great tea drinkers; but Burton, Dean Swift, Addison, Steele, Leigh Hunt, and many others celebrated coffee.

The Intervention of Mother Nature in the Coffee Plant

It is doubtful if in all nature there is a more cunningly devised food package than the fruit of the coffee tree. It seems as if Good Mother Nature had said: "This gift of Heaven is too precious to put up in any ordinary parcel. I shall design for it a casket worthy of its divine origin. And the casket shall have an inner seal that shall safeguard it from enemies, and that shall preserve its goodness for man until the day when, transported over the deserts and across the seas, it shall be broken open to be transmuted by the fires of friendship, and made to yield up its aromatic nectar in the Great Drink of Democracy."

To this end she caused to grow from the heart of the jasmine-like flower, that first herald of its coming, a marvelous berry which, as it ripens, turns first from green to yellow, then to reddish, to deep crimson, and at last to a royal purple.

The coffee fruit is very like a cherry, though somewhat elongated and having in its upper end a small umbilicus. But mark with what ingenuity the package has been constructed! The outer wrapping is a thin, gossamer-like skin which encloses a soft pulp, sweetish to the taste, but of a mucilaginous consistency. This pulp in turn is wrapped about the inner seal—called the parchment, because of its tough texture. The parchment encloses the magic bean in its last wrapping, a delicate silver-colored skin, not unlike fine spun silk or the sheerest of tissue papers. And this last wrapping is so tenacious, so true to its guardianship function, that no amount of rough treatment can dislodge it altogether; for portions of it cling to the bean even into the roasting and grinding processes.

///

Coffee Depravation

There is no reason why any person who is fond of coffee should forego its use. Paraphrasing Makaroff: Be modest, be kind, eat less, and think more, live to serve, work and play and laugh and love—it is enough! Do this and you may drink coffee without danger to your immortal soul.

The Shifting Currents of Coffee

Seldom does the coffee drinker realize how the ends of the earth are drawn upon to bring the perfected beverage to his lips. The trail that ends in his breakfast cup, if followed back, would be found to go a devious and winding way, soon splitting up into half-a-dozen or more straggling branches that would lead to as many widely scattered regions. If he could mount to a point where he could enjoy a bird's-eye view of these and a hundred kindred trails, he would find an intricate crisscross of streamlets and rivers of coffee forming a tangled pattern over the tropics and reaching out north and south to all civilized countries. This would be a picture of the coffee trade throughout the world.

It would be a motion picture, with the rivulets swelling larger at certain seasons, but seldom drying up entirely at any time. In the main, the streamlets and rivers keep pretty much the same direction and volume one year after another, but then there is also a quiet shifting of these currents. Some grow larger, and others diminish gradually until they fade out entirely. In one of the regions from which they take their source, a tree disease may cause a decline; in another, a hurricane may lay the industry low at one quick stroke; and in still another, a rival crop may drain away the life-blood of capital. But for the most part, when times are normal, the shift is gradual; for international trade is conservative, and likes to run where it finds a well-worn channel.

///

On the Intolerance of Coffee

L ike all good things in life, the drinking of coffee may be abused. Indeed, those having an idiosyncratic susceptibility to alkaloids should be temperate in the use of tea, coffee, or cocoa. In every high-tensioned country there is likely to be a small number of people who, because of certain individual characteristics, cannot drink coffee at all. These belong to the abnormal minority of the human family. Some people cannot eat strawberries; but that would not be a valid reason for a general condemnation of strawberries. One may be poisoned, says Thomas A. Edison, from too much food. Horace Fletcher was certain that overfeeding causes all our ills. Overindulgence in meat is likely to spell trouble for the strongest of us. Coffee is, perhaps, less often abused than wrongly accused. It all depends. A little more tolerance!

Coffee Quips and Bon Mots

Coffee literature is full of quips and anecdotes:

◆ An old proverb says: "To an old man a cup of coffee is like the door post of an old house—it sustains and strengthens him."

◆ Isid Bourdon said: "The discovery of coffee has enlarged the realm of illusion and given more promise to hope."

◆ Prince Talleyrand, the French diplomat and wit, has given us the cleverest summing up of the ideal cup of coffee. He said it should be "black as the devil, hot as hell, pure as an angel, sweet as love."

◆ Jean de la Roque, the French journalist, called the beverage "the King of Perfumes," whose charm was enriched when vanilla was added.

◆ The French novelist Emile Souvestre said: "Coffee keeps, so to say, the balance between bodily and spiritual nourishment."

◆ Sydney Smith, the English clergyman and humorist, once said: "If you want to improve your understanding, drink coffee; it is the intellectual beverage."

◆ Our own American William Dean Howells pays the beverage this tribute: "This coffee intoxicates without exciting, soothes you softly out of dull sobriety, making you think and talk of all the pleasant things that ever happened to you."

COFFEE'S HISTORIC ROOTS

Coffee and the Ancients

In early Grecian and Roman writings, no mention is made of either the coffee plant or the beverage made from the berries. Pierre Delia Valle (1586–1652), however, maintains that the nepenthe, which Homer says Helen brought out of Egypt and employed as surcease for sorrow, was nothing else but coffee mixed with wine. "She mingled with the wine the wondrous juice of a plant which banishes sadness and wrath from the heart and brings with it forgetfulness of every woe." Several later British authors have suggested the probability of coffee being the "black broth" of the Lacedæmonians.

Philippe Sylvester Dufour mentions as a possible objection against coffee that "the use and eating of beans were heretofore forbidden by Pythagoras," but intimates that the coffee bean of Arabia is something different.

Coffee and the Bible

George Paschius, in his Latin treatise of the *New Discoveries Made since the Time of the Ancients*, published in 1700, says he believes that coffee was meant by the five measures of parched corn included among the presents Abigail made to David to appease his wrath, as recorded in the Bible, 1 Samuel. The Vulgate translates the Hebrew words *sein kali into sata polentea*, which signify wheat, roasted or dried by fire.

Pierre Étienne Louis Dumant, the Swiss Protestant minister and author, is of the opinion that coffee (and not lentils, as others have supposed) was the red pottage for which Esau sold his birthright; also that the parched grain that Boaz ordered to be given Ruth was undoubtedly roasted coffee berries.

///

Coffee and the Koran

Still another tradition tells how the coffee drink was revealed to Mohammed himself by the Angel Gabriel. Coffee's partisans found satisfaction in a passage in the Koran which, they said, foretold its adoption by the followers of the Prophet:

> They shall be given to drink an excellent wine, sealed; its seal is that of the musk.

The most diligent research does not carry a knowledge of coffee back beyond the time of Rhazes, two hundred years after Mohammed. So there is little more than speculation or conjecture to support the theory that it was known to the ancients, in Bible times or in the days of The Praised One. Our knowledge of tea, on the other hand, antedates the Christian era. We know also that tea was intensively cultivated and taxed under the Tang dynasty in China, 793 A.D., and that Arab traders knew of it in the following century.

///

The First Appearance of Coffee in Ethiopia

While the true origin of coffee drinking may be forever hidden, shrouded as it is in legend and fable, scholars have marshaled sufficient facts to prove that the beverage was known in Ethiopia "from time immemorial," and there is much to add verisimilitude to this theory.

The coffee drink had its rise in the classical period of Arabian medicine, which dates from Abu Bakr Muhammad ibn Zakariya El Razi, called Rhazes, who followed the doctrines of Galen and sat at the feet of Hippocrates. Rhazes, who lived from 850 to 922 A.D., was the first to treat medicine in an encyclopedic manner, and, according to some authorities, the first writer to mention coffee.

Rhazes assured his readers that "bunchum (coffee) is hot and dry and very good for the stomach."

The Legend of Sheik Omar

There are several Mohammedan traditions that have persisted through the centuries, claiming the honor and glory of the first use of coffee as a beverage. One of these relates how, about 1258 A.D., Sheik Omar by chance discovered the coffee drink at Ousab in Arabia, whither he had been exiled.

One version of this legend gives it as follows:

The dervish Hadji Omar was driven by his enemies out of Mocha into the desert, where they expected he would die of starvation. This undoubtedly would have occurred if he had not plucked up the courage to taste some strange berries which he found growing on a shrub. While they seemed to be edible, they were very bitter; and he tried to improve the taste by roasting them. He found, however, that they had become very hard, so he attempted to soften them with water. The berries seemed to remain as hard as before, but the liquid turned brown, and Omar drank it on the chance that it contained some of the nourishment from the berries. He was amazed at how it refreshed him, enlivened his sluggishness, and raised his drooping spirits. Later, when he returned to Mocha, his salvation was considered a miracle. The beverage to which it was due sprang into high favor, and Omar himself was made a saint.

The Legend of the Goat Herder

The most popular coffee origin legend ascribes the discovery of the drink to an Arabian herdsman in upper Egypt, or Abyssinia, who complained to the abbot of a neighboring monastery that the goats confided to his care became unusually frolicsome after eating the berries of certain shrubs found near their feeding grounds.

The abbot, having observed the fact, determined to try the virtues of the berries on himself. He, too, responded with a new exhilaration. Accordingly, he directed that some be boiled, and the decoction drunk by his monks, who thereafter found no difficulty in keeping awake during the religious services of the night. The abbé Massieu in his poem, *Carmen Caffaeum*, thus celebrates the event:

> *The monks each in turn, as the evening draws near,*
> *Drink 'round the great cauldron—a circle of cheer!*
> *And the dawn in amaze, revisiting that shore,*
> *On idle beds of ease surprised them nevermore!*

According to the legend, the news of the "wakeful monastery" spread rapidly, and the magical berry soon "came to be in request throughout the whole kingdom; and in progress of time other nations and provinces of the East fell into the use of it."

Early Methods of Coffee Consumption

Research shows that, perhaps as early as 800 A.D., the practice of coffee consumption was started by crushing the whole ripe berries, beans and hulls, in mortars, mixing them with fats, and rounding them into food balls. Later, the dried berries were so used. The inhabitants of Groix also thrived on a diet that included roasted coffee beans.

About 900 A.D., a kind of aromatic wine was made in Africa from the fermented juice of the hulls and pulp of the ripe berries. The first coffee drinkers did not think of roasting but, impressed by the aroma of the dried beans, they put them in cold water and drank the liquor saturated with their aromatic principles. Crushing the raw beans and hulls, and steeping them in water, was a later improvement.

It appears that boiled coffee (the name is *anathema* today) was invented about the year 1000 A.D. Even then, the beans were not roasted. We read of their use in medicine in the form of a decoction. The dried fruit, beans and hulls, were boiled in stone or clay cauldrons. The custom of using the sun-dried hulls, without roasting, still exists in Africa, Arabia, and parts of southern Asia. Inhabitants of Sumatra neglect the fruit of the coffee tree and use the leaves to make a tea-like infusion. Édelestan Jardin, who published *Le Caféier et le Caféin* Paris in 1895, relates that in Guiana an agreeable tea is made by drying the young buds of the coffee tree and rolling them on a copper plate slightly heated. In Uganda, the inhabitants eat the raw berries; from bananas and coffee they make also a sweet, savory drink which is called *menghai*.

//

The Spread of Coffee in the Middle East

About 1454 A.D., Sheik Gemaleddin Abou Muhammad Bensaid, mufti of Aden, a small town where he was born, became acquainted with the virtues of coffee on a journey into Abyssinia (Ethiopia). Upon his return to Aden, his health became impaired; and remembering the coffee he had seen his countrymen drinking in Abyssinia, he sent for some in the hope of finding relief. He not only recovered from his illness, but because of its sleep-dispelling qualities, he sanctioned the use of the drink among the dervishes "that they might spend the night in prayers or other religious exercises with more attention and presence of mind."

It is altogether probable that the coffee drink was known in Aden before the time of Sheik Gemaleddin, but the endorsement of the very learned imam, whom science and religion had already made famous, was sufficient to start a vogue for the beverage that spread throughout Yemen, and then to the far corners of the world. We read in the Arabian manuscript at the *Bibliothéque Nationale* that lawyers, students, artisans, and others who worked at night, to escape the heat of the day, took to drinking coffee.

Coffee Baptized by the Pope

Shortly after coffee reached Rome, according to a much quoted legend, it was threatened with religious fanaticism, which almost caused its excommunication from Christendom. It is related that certain priests appealed to Pope Clement VIII (1535–1605) to have its use forbidden among Christians, denouncing it as an invention of Satan. For Christians to drink coffee, they claimed, was to risk falling into a trap set by Satan for their souls.

The pope, made curious, desired to inspect this Devil's drink, and had some brought to him. The aroma of it was so pleasant and inviting that the pope was tempted to try a cupful. After drinking it, he exclaimed, "Why, this Satan's drink is so delicious that it would be a pity to let the infidels have exclusive use of it. We shall fool Satan by baptizing it, and making it a truly Christian beverage."

Thus, whatever harmfulness its opponents try to attribute to coffee, the fact remains (if we are to credit the story) that it has been baptized and proclaimed harmless, and a "truly Christian beverage," by his holiness the pope.

Coffee and Famous Frenchmen

Louis XV had a great passion for coffee, which he made himself. Lenormand, the head gardener at Versailles, raised six pounds of coffee a year, which was for the exclusive use of the king. The king's fondness for coffee and for Mme. Du Barry gave rise to a celebrated anecdote of Louveciennes, which was accepted as true by many serious writers. It is told in this fashion by Mairobert in a pamphlet scandalizing Du Barry in 1776:

His Majesty loves to make his own coffee and to forsake the cares of the government. One day the coffee pot was on the fire and, his Majesty being occupied with something else, the coffee boiled over. "Oh

France, take care! Your coffee *fout le camp!*" (colorful language for "taking off" or "buggering off") cried the beautiful favorite. ●

It is related of Jean Jacques Rousseau that once when he was walking in the Tuileries, he caught the aroma of roasting coffee. Turning to his companion, Bernardino de Saint-Pierre, he said, "Ah, that is a perfume in which I delight; when they roast coffee near my house, I hasten to open the door to take in all the aroma." And such was the passion for coffee of this philosopher of Geneva that when he died, "he just missed doing it with a cup of coffee in his hand."

●

Barthez, confidential physician of Napoleon the First, drank a great deal of it, freely, calling it "the intellectual drink." Bonaparte himself said: "Strong coffee, and plenty, awakens me. It gives me a warmth, an unusual force, a pain that is not without pleasure. I would rather suffer than be senseless."

The Duel for Coffee's Honor

One day while M. Saint-Foix, a French playwright, was seated at his usual table in Café Procope in Paris, an officer of the king's bodyguard entered, sat down, and ordered a cup of coffee, with milk and a roll, adding, "It will serve me for a dinner."

At this, Saint-Foix remarked aloud that a cup of coffee, with milk and a roll, was a confoundedly poor dinner. The officer remonstrated. Saint-Foix reiterated his remark, adding that nothing he could say to the contrary would convince him that it was not a confoundedly poor dinner.

Thereupon a challenge was given and accepted, and the whole company present adjourned as spectators to a duel which ended by Saint-Foix receiving a wound in the arm.

"That is all very well," said the wounded combatant; "but I call you to witness, gentlemen, that I am still profoundly convinced that a cup of coffee, with milk and a roll, is a confoundedly poor dinner."

At this moment the principals were arrested and carried before the Duke de Noailles, in whose presence Saint-Foix, without waiting to be questioned, said, "Monseigneur, I had not the slightest intention of offending this gallant officer who, I doubt not, is an honorable man; but your excellency can never prevent my asserting that a cup of coffee, with milk and a roll, is a confoundedly poor dinner."

"Why, so it is," said the Duke.

"Then I am not in the wrong," persisted Saint-Foix; "and a cup of coffee"—at these words magistrates, delinquents, and auditory burst into a roar of laughter, and the antagonists forthwith became warm friends.

Coffee and the Chancellor of the German Empire

Among coffee drinkers a high place must be given to Otto Von Bismarck, who lived from 1815 until 1898. He liked coffee pure and unadulterated, without the chicory that many would use as a filler.

While with the Prussian army in France, he one day entered a country inn and asked the host if he had any chicory in the house. He had. Bismarck said: "Well, bring it to me; all you have." The man obeyed, and handed Bismarck a canister full of chicory.

"Are you sure this is all you have?" demanded the chancellor.

"Yes, my lord, every grain."

"Then," said Bismarck, keeping the canister by him, "go now and make me a pot of coffee."

The First English Mention of Coffee

In 1599, Sir Antony (or Anthony) Sherley, a picturesque gentleman-adventurer, the first Englishman to mention coffee drinking in the Orient, sailed from Venice on a kind of self-appointed, informal Persian mission, to invite the shah to ally himself with the Christian princes against the Turks, and incidentally, to promote English trade interests in the East. The English government knew nothing of the arrangement, disavowed him, and forbade his return to England. However, the expedition got to Persia; and the account of the voyage thither was written by William Parry, one of the Sherley party, and was published in London in 1601. It is interesting because it contains the first printed reference to coffee in English, employing the more modern form of the word.

The passage is part of an account of the manners and customs of the Turkish in Aleppo. It reads:

> They sit at their meat (which is served to them upon the ground) as Tailers sit upon their stalls, crosse-legd; for the most part, passing the day in banqueting and carowsing, untill they surfet, drinking a certaine liquor, which they do call Coffe, which is made of seede much like mustard seede, which will soone intoxicate the braine.

Biddulph's description of the drink, and of the coffee-house customs of the Turks, was the first detailed account to be written by an Englishman. It also appears in *Purchas His Pilgrimes* published in 1625. To quote:

Their most common drinke is Coffa, which is a blacke kinde of drinke, made of a kind of Pulse like Pease, called Coaua; which being grownd in the Mill, and boiled in water, they drinke it as hot as they can suffer it; which they finde to agree very well with them against their crudities, and feeding on hearbs and rawe meates. Other compounded drinkes they have, called Sherbet, made of Water and Sugar, or Hony, with Snow therein to make it coole; for although the Countrey bee hot, yet they keepe Snow all the yeere long to coole their drinke. It is accounted a great curtesie amongst them to give unto their frends when they come to visit them, a Finion or Scudella of Coffa, which is more holesome than toothsome, for it causeth good concoction, and driveth away drowsinesse.

Some of them will also drinke Bersh or Opium, which maketh them forget themselves, and talk idely of Castles in the Ayre, as though they saw Visions, and heard Revelations. Their Coffa houses are more common than Ale-houses in England; but they use not so much to sit in the houses, as on benches on both sides the streets, neere unto a Coffa house, every man with his Fin-ionful; which being smoking hot, they use to put it to their Noses & Eares, and then sup it off by leasure, being full of idle and Ale-house talke whiles they are amongst themselves drinking it; if there be any news, it is talked of there.

Introduction of Coffee to England

Although it seems likely that coffee must have been introduced into England sometime during the first quarter of the seventeenth century, with so many writers and travelers describing it, and with so much trading going on between the merchants of the British Isles and the Orient, yet the first reliable record we have of its advent is to be found in the *Diary and Correspondence of John Evelyn, F.R.S.*, where he says:

> There came in my time to the college (Baliol, Oxford) one Nathaniel Conopios, out of Greece, from Cyrill, the Patriarch of Constantinople, who, returning many years after was made (as I understand) Bishop of Smyrna. He was the first I ever saw drink coffee; which custom came not into England till thirty years thereafter.

Evelyn should have said thirteen years after; for then it was that the first coffee house was opened, in 1650.

Conopios was a native of Crete, trained in the Greek church. He became primore to Cyrill, Patriarch of Constantinople. When Cyrill was strangled by the vizier, Conopios fled to England to avoid a like barbarity. He came with credentials to Archbishop Laud, who allowed him maintenance in Balliol College.

It was observed that while he continued in Balliol College he made the drink for his own use called Coffey, and usually drank it every morning, being the first, as the antients of that House have informed me, that was ever drank in Oxon. 🫘

THE
COFFEE
TRADE

Three Centuries of Coffee Trading

The story of the development of the world's coffee trade is a story of about three centuries. When Columbus sailed for the new world, the coffee plant was unknown even as near its original home as his native Italy. In its probable birthplace in southern Abyssinia, the inhabitants had enjoyed its use for a long time, and it had spread to southwestern Arabia; but the Mediterranean knew nothing of it until after the beginning of the sixteenth century. It then crept slowly along the coast of Asia Minor, through Syria, Damascus, and Aleppo, until it reached Constantinople in about 1554. It became very popular; coffee houses were opened, and the first of many controversies arose. But coffee made its way against all opposition, and soon was firmly established in Turkish territory.

In those deliberate times, the next step westward, from Asia to Europe, was not taken for more than fifty years. In general, its introduction and establishment in Europe occupied the whole of the seventeenth century.

The greatest pioneering work in coffee trading was done by the Netherlands East India Company, which began operations in 1602. The enterprise not only promoted the spread of coffee growing in two hemispheres; but it was active also in introducing the sale of the product in many European countries.

Coffee reached Venice in about 1615, and Marseilles in about 1644. The French began importing coffee in commercial quantities in 1660. The Dutch began to import Mocha coffee regularly in Amsterdam in 1663; and by 1679 the French had developed a considerable trade in the berry between the Levant and the cities of Lyons and Marseilles. Meanwhile, the coffee drink had become fashionable in Paris, partly through its use by the Turkish ambassador, and the first Parisian café was opened in 1672. It is significant of its steady popularity since then that the name café, which is both French and Spanish for coffee, has come to mean a general eating or drinking place.

Since the spread of the use of coffee to western Europe in the seventeenth century, the development of the trade has been marked, broadly speaking, by two features:

1. The shifting of the weight of production, first to the West Indies, then to the East Indies, and then to Brazil.
2. The rise of the United States as the chief coffee consumer of the world.

Until the close of the seventeenth century, the little district in Arabia, whence the coffee beans had first made their way to Europe, continued to supply the whole world's trade. But sprigs of coffee trees were beginning to go out from Arabia to other promising lands, both eastward and westward.

The year 1699 was an important one in the history of this expansion, as it was then that the Dutch successfully introduced the coffee plant from Arabia into Java. This started a Far Eastern industry, whose importance continues to this day, and also caused the mother country, Holland, to take up the role of one of the leading coffee traders of the world.

Holland, in fact, took to coffee from the very first. It is claimed that the first samples were introduced into that country from Mocha in 1616—long before the beans were known in England or France—and that by 1663, regular shipments were being made. Soon after the coffee culture became firmly established in Java, regular shipments to the mother country began, the first of these being a consignment of 894 pounds in 1711. Under the auspices of the Netherlands East India Co. the system of cultivating coffee by forced labor was begun in the East Indian colonies. It flourished until well into the nineteenth century.

The introduction of the coffee plant into the new world took place between 1715 and 1723. It quickly spread to the islands and the mainland washed by the Caribbean. The latter part of the eighteenth century saw tens of millions of pounds of coffee being shipped yearly to the mother countries of western Europe; and for decades, the two great coffee trade currents of the world continued to run from the West Indies to France, England, Holland, and Germany; and from the Dutch East Indies to Holland. These currents continued to flow until the disruption of world trade routes by the World War; but they had been pushed into positions of secondary importance by the establishing of two new currents, running respectively from Brazil to Europe, and from Brazil to the United States, which constituted the nineteenth century's contribution to the history of the world's coffee trade.

The rise of Brazil to the place of all-important source of the world's coffee was entirely a nineteenth-century development. When the coffee tree found its true home in southern Brazil in 1770, it began at once to spread widely over the area of excellent soil; but there was little exportation for thirty or forty years. By the middle of the nineteenth century, Brazil was contributing twice as much to the world's commerce as her nearest competitor, the Dutch East Indies.

The chief feature of the twentieth century's developments has been the passing by the United States of the halfway mark in world consumption; this country, since the second year of the World War, having taken more than all the rest of the world put together. The world's chief coffee "stream," so to speak, is now from Santos and Rio de Janeiro to New York, other lesser streams being from these ports to Havre, Antwerp, Amsterdam, and Hamburg; and from Java to Amsterdam and Rotterdam.

Coffee Production

The world's yearly production of coffee is, on the average, considerably more than 1 million tons. If this were all made up into the refreshing drink we get at our breakfast tables, there would be enough to supply every inhabitant of the earth with some sixty cups a year, representing a total of more than 90 billion cups. In terms of pounds, the annual world output amounts to about 2¼ billion—an amount so large that if it were done up in the familiar one-pound paper packages, and if these packages were laid end to end in a row, they would form a line long enough to reach to the moon. If this average yearly production were left in the sacks in which the coffee is shipped, the total of 17,500,000 would be enough to form a broad, six-foot pavement reaching entirely across the United States, upon which a man could walk steadily for more than five months at the rate of twenty miles a day. This vast amount of coffee comes very largely from the western hemisphere; and about three-fourths of it is from a single country.

Brazil produces more than all the rest of the world put together. The production, shipment, and preparation of this coffee directly and indirectly supports millions of workers; and many countries are entirely dependent on it for their prosperity and economic well-being.

Coffee Consumption

Of the million or more tons of coffee produced in the world each year, practically all—with the exception of that which is used in the coffee-growing countries themselves—is consumed by the United States and western Europe, the British dominions, and the nonproducing countries of South America. Over that vast stretch of territory beginning with western Russia and extending over almost the whole of Asia, coffee is very little-known. In the consuming regions mentioned, moreover, consumption is concentrated in a few countries, which together account for some 90 percent of all the coffee that enters the world's markets. These are: the United States, which now takes more than one-half, Germany, France, Spain, Italy, Holland, Belgium, Switzerland, and Scandinavia.

COFFEE CUSTOMS IN EUROPE

France

French: *café*

Were it not for the almost inevitable high roast and the frequently disconcerting chicory addition, coffee in France might be an unalloyed delight—at least this is how it appears to American eyes. One seldom, if ever, finds coffee improperly brewed in France—it is never boiled.

Second only to the United States, France consumes about 2 million bags of coffee annually. The varieties include: coffee from the East Indies, Mocha, Haitian (a great favorite), Central American, Colombian, and Brazilian.

Although there are many wholesale and retail coffee roasters in France, home roasting persists, particularly in the country districts. The little sheet-iron cylinder roasters, that are hand-turned over an iron box holding the charcoal fire, find a ready sale even in the modern department stores of the big cities. In any village or city in France, it is a common sight on a pleasant day to find the householder turning his roaster on the curb in front of his home. Emmet G. Beeson, in the *Tea and Coffee Trade Journal*, gives us this vignette of rural coffee roasting in the south of France:

In a certain town in the south of France I saw an old man with an outfit a little larger than the home variety, a machine with a capacity of about ten pounds. Instead of a cylinder in which to roast his coffee, he had perched on a sheet-iron frame a hollow round ball made of sheet iron. In the top of this ball there was a little slide, which was opened by the means of a metal tool. In the sheet-iron frame he had kindled his charcoal fire. Directly in front of his roaster was a homemade cooling pan, the sides of which were of wood, the bottom covered with a fine grade of wire screening.

On this particular afternoon, the old man had taken up his place on the curb; and a big black cat had taken advantage of the warmth offered by the charcoal fire and was curled up, sleeping peacefully in the pan nearest the fire. The old man paid no attention to the cat, but went on rotating his ball of coffee and puffing away pensively on his cigarette. When his coffee had become blackened and burned, and blackened and burned it was, he stopped rotating the ball, opened the slide in the top, turned it over, and the hot, burned coffee rolled out, and much to his delight, on the sleeping cat, which leaped out of the pan and scampered up the street and into a hole under an old building.

I afterward learned that this old fellow made a business of going about the town gathering up coffee from the houses along the way and roasting it at a few sous per kilo.

Nearly all the coffee is ground at home, which is not a bad practice for the consumer; but perhaps is a financial hardship for the dealer, who can mix some grade grinders into his blends without doing them any material harm. Where coffee mills are used in the stores, they are of the Strong-Arm family and of an ancient heritage. To get a growl out of the grocer in France, buy a kilo of coffee and ask him to grind it.

Packaged coffee and proprietary brands have not come into their own to the extent that they have in the United States, although there are at present two firms in Paris which have started in this business and are advertising extensively on billboards, in streetcars, and in the subways. However, most coffee is still sold in bulk. The butter, egg, and cheese stores of France do a very large business in coffee. Prior to the war and high prices, there were some very large firms doing a premium business in coffee, tea, spices, etc. They still exist, and have a very fine trade; but since the high prices of coffees and premiums, the business has gone down very materially. They operate by the wagon route and solicitor method, just as some of our American companies do. One very large firm in Paris has been in this business for more than thirty years, operating branches and wagons in every town, village, and hamlet in France.

The consumption of coffee is increasing very materially in France, some say, on account of the high price of wine; others hold that coffee is simply growing in favor with the people. Among the masses, French breakfast consists of a bowl or cup of *café au lait*, or half a cup or bowl of strong black coffee and chicory, and

half a cup of hot milk, and a yard of bread. The work-
ingman turns his bread on end and inserts it into his
bowl of coffee, allowing it to soak up as much of the
liquid as possible. Then he proceeds to suck this concoction into his system. His approval is demonstrated
by the amount of noise he makes in the operation.

Among the better classes, the breakfast is the same:
café au lait, with rolls and butter, and sometimes fruit.
The brew is prepared by the drip, or true percolator,
method, or by filtration. Boiling milk is poured into
the cup from a pot held in one hand together with
the brewed coffee from a pot held in the other, pro-
viding a simultaneous mixture. The proportions vary
from half-and-half to one part coffee and three parts
milk. Sometimes, the service is given by pouring into
the cup a little coffee, then the same quantity of milk,
and alternating in this way until the cup is filled.

Coffee is never drunk with any meal but breakfast,
but is invariably served *en demi-tasse* after the noon and
the evening meals. In the home, the usual thing after
luncheon or dinner is to go into the salon and have
your *demi-tasse*, liqueur, and cigarettes before a cozy
grate fire. A Frenchman's idea of after-dinner coffee is
a brew that is unusually thick and black, and he invariably takes with it his liqueur, no matter if he has had
a cocktail for an appetizer, a bottle of red wine with
his meat course, and a bottle of white wine with the
salad and dessert courses. When the *demi-tasse* comes
along, with it must be served his cordial in the shape

of cognac, benedictine, or crème de menthe. He cannot conceive of a man not taking a little alcohol with his after-dinner coffee, as an aid, he says, to digestion.

Making coffee in France has been, and always will be, by the drip and the filtration methods. The large hotels and cafés follow these methods almost entirely, and so does the housewife. When company comes, and something unusual in coffee is to be served, Mr. Beeson says he has known the cook to drip the coffee, using a spoonful of hot water at a time, pouring it over tightly packed, finely ground coffee, allowing the water to percolate through to extract every particle of oil. They use more ground coffee in bulk than they get liquid in the cup, and sometimes spend an hour producing four or five *demi-tasses*. It is needless to say that it is more like molasses than coffee when ready for drinking.

It is not unusual in some parts of France to save the coffee grounds for a second or even a third infusion, but this is not considered good practice.

Von Liebig's idea of correct coffee making (found in the later section on Germany's coffee customs) has been adapted to French practice in some instances after this fashion: Put used coffee grounds in the bottom chamber of a drip coffee pot. Put freshly ground coffee in the upper chamber. Pour on boiling water. The theory is that the old coffee furnishes body and strength, and the fresh coffee the aroma.

The cafés that line the boulevards of Paris and the larger cities of France all serve coffee, either plain or with milk, and almost always with liqueur. The coffee house in France may be said to be the wine house; or the wine house may be said to be the coffee house. They are inseparable. In the smallest or the largest of these establishments, coffee can be had at any time of day or night. The proprietor of a very large café in Paris says his coffee sales during the day almost equal his wine sales.

In the afternoon, café means a small cup or glass of *café noir*, or *café nature*. It is double the usual amount of coffee dripped by percolator or filtration device, the process consuming eight to ten minutes. Some understand *café noir* to mean equal parts of coffee and brandy with sugar and vanilla to taste. When *café noir* is mixed with an equal quantity of cognac alone, it becomes *café gloria*. *Café mazagran* is also much in demand in the summertime. The coffee base is made as for *café noir*, and it is served in a tall glass with water to dilute it to one's taste.

Germany

German: *kaffee* (coffee tree: *kaffeebaum*)

Germany originated the afternoon coffee function known as the *kaffee-klatsch*. Even today, the German family's reunion takes place around the coffee table on Sunday afternoons. In summer, when weather permits, the family will take a walk into the suburbs, and stop at a garden where coffee is sold in pots. The proprietor furnishes the coffee, the cups, the spoons, and, in normal times, the sugar, two pieces to each cup. The patrons bring their own cake. They put one piece of sugar into each cup and take the other pieces home to the "canary bird," meaning the sugar bowl in the pantry.

Baron Von Liebig's method of making coffee, whereby three-fourths of the quantity to be used is first boiled for ten or fifteen minutes, and the remainder added for a six-minute steeping or infusion, is religiously followed by some housekeepers. Von Liebig advocated coating the bean with sugar. In some families, fats, eggs, and eggshells are used to settle and to clarify the beverage.

Coffee in Germany is better cooked (roasted) and more scientifically prepared than in many other European countries. In recent years, during the World War and since, however, there has been an amazing increase in the use of coffee substitutes, so that the German cup of coffee is not the pure delight it was once.

Cheaper coffee is served in some gardens, which conspicuously display large signs at the entrance, saying: "Families may cook their own coffee in this place." In such a garden, the patron merely buys the hot water from the proprietor, furnishing the ground coffee and cake himself.

While waiting for the coffee to brew, he may listen to the band and watch the children play under the trees. French or Vienna drip pots are used for brewing.

Every city in Germany has its cafés, spacious places where patrons sit around small tables, drinking coffee, "with or without," turned or unturned, steaming or iced, sweetened or unsweetened, depending on the sugar supply; nibble, at the same time, a piece of cake or pastry, selected from a glass pyramid; talk, flirt, malign, yawn, read, and smoke. Cafés are, in fact, public reading rooms. Some places keep hundreds of daily and weekly newspapers and magazines on file for the use of patrons. If the customer buys only one cup of coffee, he may keep his seat for hours and read one newspaper after another.

The United Kingdom

In the British Isles, coffee is still being boiled; although the infusion, true percolation (drip), and filtration methods have many advocates. A favorite device is the earthenware jug with or without the cotton sack that makes it a coffee biggin. When used without the sack, the best practice is first to warm the jug. For each pint of liquor, one ounce (three dessert-spoonfuls) of freshly ground coffee is put in the pot. Upon it is poured freshly boiling water—three-fourths of the amount required. After stirring with a wooden spoon, the remainder of the water is poured in, and the pot is returned to the "hob" to infuse, and to settle for three to five minutes. Some stir it a second time before the final settling.

From an American point of view, the principal defects in the English method of making coffee lie in the roasting, handling, and brewing. It has been charged that the beans are not properly cooked in the first place, and that they are too often stale before being ground. The English run to a light or cinnamon roast, whereas the best American practice requires a medium, high, or city roast. A fairly high shade of brown is favored on the South Downs with a light shade for Lancashire, the West Riding of Yorkshire, and the south of Scotland. The trade demands, for the most part, a ripe chestnut brown. Wholesale roasting is done by gas and coke machines; while retail dealers use mostly a small type of inner-heated gas machine.

The British consumer will need much instruction before the national character of the beverage shows a uniform improvement. While the coffee may be more carefully roasted, better "cooked" than it was formerly, it is still remaining too long unsold after roasting, or else it is being ground too long a time before making. These abuses are, however, being corrected; and the consumer is everywhere being urged to buy his coffee freshly roasted and to have it freshly ground. Another factor has undoubtedly contributed to giving England a bad name among lovers of good coffee, and that is certain tinned "coffees," composed of ground coffee and chicory, mixtures that attained some vogue for a time as "French" coffee. They found favor, perhaps, because they were easily handled. Packaged coffees have not been developed in England as in America; but there is a more or less limited field for them, and there are several good brands of absolutely pure coffee on the market.

The *demi-tasse* is a popular drink after luncheon, after dinner, and even during the day, especially in the cities. In London, there are cafés that make a specialty of it.

While, in the home it is customary to steep the coffee; in hotels and restaurants, some form of percolating apparatus, extractor, or steam machine is employed.

American visitors complain that coffee in England is too thick and syrupy for their liking. Coffee in restaurants is served "white" (with milk) or black, in earthen stoneware or silver pots. In chain restaurants, one can find on the menu "hot milk with a dash of coffee."

The steeping method so much favored in England may be responsible for some of the unkind things said about English coffee; because it undoubtedly leads to the abuse of over-infusion, so that the net result is as bad as boiling.

The vast majority of English people are, however, confirmed tea drinkers, and it is extremely doubtful if this national habit, ingrained through centuries of use of "the cup that cheers" at breakfast and at tea time in the afternoon, can ever be changed.

The London coffee houses of the seventeenth and eighteenth centuries gave way to a type of coffee house whose mainstay was its food rather than its drink. In time, these too began to yield to the changing influences of a civilization that demanded modern hotels, luxurious tea lounges, smart restaurants, chain shops, tea rooms, and cafés with and without coffee. A certain type of "coffee shop," with rough boarded stalls, sanded floors, and "private rooms," frequented by lower class workingmen, were to be found in England for a time; but because of their doubtful character, they were closed up by the police.

Italy

Italian: *caffè*

In Italy, coffee is roasted in a wholesale and retail way as well as in the home. French, German, Dutch, and Italian machines are used. The full city, or Italian, roast is favored. There are cafés as in other continental countries, and the drink is prepared in the French fashion. For restaurants and hotels, rapid filtering machines, first developed by the French and Italians, are used. In the home, percolators and filtration devices are employed.

The De Mattia Brothers have a process designed to conserve the aroma in roasting. The Italians pay particular attention to the temperature in roasting and in the cooling operation. There is considerable glazing, and many coffee additions are used.

Like the French, the Italians make much of *café au lait* for breakfast. At dinner, the *café noir* is served.

Greece

Greek: *kaféo*

Coffee is the most popular and most extensively used nonalcoholic beverage in Greece. Its annual per capita consumption there is about two pounds, two-thirds of the supply coming via Austria and France, Brazil furnishing directly the bulk of the remaining third.

Coffee is given a high or city roast, and is used almost entirely in powdered form. It is prepared for consumption principally in the Turkish *demi-tasse* way. Finely ground coffee is used even in making ordinary table or breakfast coffee. In private houses the cylindrical brass hand-grinders, manufactured in Constantinople, are mostly used. In many of the coffee houses in the villages and country towns throughout Greece, a heavy iron pestle, wielded by a strong man, is employed to pulverize the grains in a heavy stone or marble mortar; while the poorer homes use a small brass pestle and mortar, also manufactured in Turkey.

In his work *The Greeks of the Present Day*, Edmond François Valentin About says:

> The coffee which is drunk in all the Greek houses rather astonishes the travellers who have neither seen Turkey nor Algeria. One is surprised at finding food in a cup in which one expected drink. Yet you get accustomed to this coffee-broth and end by finding it

more savoury, lighter, more perfumed, and especially more wholesome, than the extract of coffee you
drink in France.

Then About gives the recipe of his servant Petros, who
is "the first man in Athens for coffee":

The grain is roasted without burning it; it is reduced
to an impalpable powder, either in a mortar or in a
very close-grained mill. Water is set on the fire till
it boils up; it is taken off to throw in a spoonful of
coffee, and a spoonful of pounded sugar for each cup
it is intended to make; it is carefully mixed; the coffee pot is replaced on the fire until the contents seem
ready to boil over; it is taken off, and set on again;
lastly it is quickly poured into the cups. Some coffee drinkers have this preparation boiled as many as
five times. Petros makes a rule of not putting his
coffee more than three times on the fire. He takes
care in filling the cups to divide impartially the co-
loured froth which rises above the coffee pot; it is
the kaimaki of the coffee. A cup without kaimaki is
disgraced.

When the coffee is poured out you are at liberty
to drink it boiling and muddy, or cold and clear. Real
amateurs drink it without waiting. Those who allow
the sediment to settle down, do not do so from con-
tempt, for they afterwards collect it with the little
finger and eat it carefully.

Thus prepared, coffee may be taken without in-convenience ten times a day: five cups of French cof-fee could not be drunk with impunity every day. It is because the coffee of the Turks and the Greeks is a diluted tonic, and ours is a concentrated tonic. ☕

The Netherlands

Dutch: *koffie* **(coffee tree:** *koffieboonen***)**

In the Netherlands, the French café is a delightful fea-ture of the life of the larger cities. The Dutch roast coffee properly, and make it well. The service is in in-dividual pots, or in *demi-tasses* on a silver, nickel, or brass tray, and accompanied by a miniature pitcher containing just enough cream (usually whipped), a small dish about the size of an individual butter plate holding three squares of sugar, and a slender glass of water. This service is universal; the glass of water al-ways goes with the coffee. It is the one sure way for Americans to get a drink of water. It is the custom in Holland to repair to some open-air café or indoor coffee house for the after-dinner cup of coffee. One seldom takes his coffee in the place where he has his dinner. These cafés are many, and some are elaborately designed and furnished. The approved way of making coffee in Holland is the French drip method.

Russia

Russian: *kophe*

Russia drinks more tea than coffee, which is prepared in Turkish fashion by the masses, when obtainable. Usually the coffee is only a cheap "substitute." The so-called *café à la Russe* of the aristocracy is strong black coffee flavored with lemon. Another Russian recipe calls for the coffee to be placed in a large punch bowl, and covered with a layer of finely chopped apples and pears; then cognac is poured over the mass, and a match applied.

Austria

German: *kaffee* (coffee tree: *kaffeebaum*)

Coffee is made in Austria after the French style, usually by the drip method or in the pumping percolator device, commonly called the Vienna coffee machine. The restaurants employ a large-sized urn fitted with a combination metal sieve and cloth sack. After the ground coffee has infused for about six minutes, a screw device raises the metal sieve, the pressure forcing the liquid through the cloth sack containing the ground coffee.

Vienna cafés are famous, but the World War has dimmed their glory. It used to be said that their equal could not be found for general excellence and moderate prices. From half-past eight to ten in the morning, large numbers of people were wont to breakfast in them on a cup of coffee or tea, with a roll and butter. *Mélangé* is with milk; "brown" coffee is darker; and *a schwarzer* is without milk. In all the cafés, the visitor may obtain coffee, tea, liqueurs, ices, bottled beer, ham, eggs, etc. Then there are the dairies with coffee, a unique institution.

For Vienna coffee, the liquor is usually made in a pumping percolator or by the drip process. In normal times, it is served two parts coffee to one of hot milk and topped with whipped cream. During 1914–18 and the recent postwar period, however, the sparkling crown of delicious whipped cream gave way to condensed milk, and saccharine took the place of sugar.

///

Spain

Spanish: *café*

In Spain, the French type of café flourishes. In Madrid, some delightful cafés are to be found around the Puerto del Sol, where coffee and chocolate are the favorite drinks. The coffee is made by the drip process, and is served in French fashion.

Norway and Sweden

Norwegian and Swedish: *kaffe*

French and German influences mark the roasting, grinding, preparing, and serving of coffee in Norway and Sweden. Generally speaking, not so much chicory is used, and a great deal of whipped cream is employed. In Norway, the boiling method has many followers. A big (open) copper kettle is used. This is filled with water, and the coffee is dumped in and boiled. In the poorer-class country homes, the copper kettle is brought to the table and set upon a wooden plate. The coffee is served directly from the kettle in cups. In better-class homes, the coffee is poured from the kettle into silver coffee pots in the kitchen, and the silver coffee pots are brought to the table. The only thing approaching coffee houses are the "coffee rooms" which are to be found in Christiania. These are small, one-room affairs in which the plainer sorts of foods, such as porridge, may be purchased with the coffee. They are cheap, and are largely frequented by the poorer class of students, who use them as places in which to study while they drink their coffee.

COFFEE
CUSTOMS
IN THE
AMERICAS

Argentina

Spanish: *café*

Coffee is very popular as a beverage in Argentina. *Café con léche*—coffee with milk, in which the proportion of coffee may vary from one-fourth to two-thirds—is the usual Argentine breakfast beverage. A small cup of coffee is generally taken after meals, and it is also consumed to a considerable extent in cafés.

Brazil

Portuguese: *café*

In Brazil, everyone drinks coffee and at all hours. Cafés making a specialty of the beverage, and modeled after continental originals, are to be found aplenty in Rio de Janeiro, Santos, and other large cities. The custom prevails of roasting the beans high, almost to carbonization, grinding them fine, and then boiling after the Turkish fashion, percolating in French drip pots, steeping in cold water for several hours, straining and heating the liquid for use as needed, or filtering by means of conical linen sacks suspended from wire rings.

The Brazilian loves to frequent cafés and to sip his coffee at his ease. He is very continental in this respect.

The wide-open doors, and the round-topped marble tables, with their small cups and saucers set around a sugar basin, make inviting pictures. The customer pulls toward him one of the cups and immediately a waiter comes and fills it with coffee, the charge for which is about three cents. It is a common thing for a Brazilian to consume one dozen to two dozen cups of black coffee a day. If one pays a social visit, calls upon the president of the Republic, or any lesser official, or on a business acquaintance, it is a signal for an attendant to serve coffee. *Café au lait* is popular in the morning; but except for this service, milk or cream is never used. In Brazil, coffee is a symbol of hospitality.

///

Canada

In Canada, we find both French and English influences at work in the preparation and serving of the beverage; "Yankee" ideas also have entered from across the border. Some years back (about 1910) A. McGill, chief chemist of the Canadian Inland Revenue Department, suggested an improvement upon Baron von Liebig's method, whereby Canadians might obtain an ideal cup of coffee. It was to combine two well-known methods. One was to boil a quantity of ground coffee to get a maximum of body or soluble matter. The other was to percolate a similar quantity to get the needed caffeol. By combining the decoction and the infusion, a finished beverage rich in body and aroma might be had. Most Canadians continue to drink tea, however, although coffee consumption is increasing.

Mexico

Spanish: *café*

In Mexico, the inhabitants have a custom of their own. The roasted beans are pounded to a powder in a cloth bag, which is then immersed in a pot of boiling water and milk. The vaquero, however, pours boiling water on the powdered coffee in his drinking cup, and sweetens it with a brown sugar stick.

Among the upper classes in Mexico, the following interesting method is used for making coffee:

Roast one pound until the beans are brown inside. Mix with the roasted coffee one teaspoonful of butter, one of sugar, and a little brandy. Cover with a thick cloth. Cool for one hour; then grind. Boil one quart of water. When boiling, put in the coffee and remove from fire immediately. Let it stand a few hours, and strain through a flannel bag, and keep in a stone jar until required for use; then heat quantity required.

COFFEE CUSTOMS IN AFRICA AND THE NEAR AND FAR EAST

Africa

Abyssinian: *bonn*

Among the inhabitants, many mix their pulverized coffee beans with fats as a food ration, and others favor the *kisher*, or beverage made from the toasted coffee hulls. An hour's boiling produces a straw-colored decoction, of a slightly sweetish taste. Adaptations of the French sidewalk café, and of the Turkish coffee house, may be seen in the larger towns.

Individual earthen vessels for making coffee, painted red and yellow, are made by some of the native tribes in Ethiopia, and usually accompany disciples of Islam when they journey to Mecca, where the vessels find a ready sale among the pilgrims, most of whom are coffee devotees.

//

The Arabian Peninsula

Arabic: *qahwah* (coffee berry: *bun*)
Turkish: *kahué*

This area deserves to be called "the Blest," if only for its gift of coffee to the world. Here it was that the virtues of the drink were first made known; here the plant first received intensive cultivation.

Several rounds of coffee, without milk or sugar, but sometimes flavored with cardamom seeds, are served to the guest at their first welcome; and coffee may be had at all hours between meals, or whenever the occasion demands it. Always the beans are freshly roasted, pounded, and boiled. The Arabs average twenty-five to thirty cups a day. Everywhere in Arabia there are to be found cafés where the beverage may be bought.

The Arab drinks water before taking coffee, but never after it. "Once in Syria," says a traveler, "I was recognized as a foreigner because I asked for water just after I had taken my coffee. 'If you belonged here,' said the waiter, 'you would not spoil the taste of coffee in your mouth by washing it away with water.'"

Originally the Turkish method of preparing coffee was the Arabian method, and it is so described by Mr. Fellows in his *Excursions Through Asia Minor*:

Each cup is made separately, the little saucepan or ladle in which it is prepared being about an inch wide and two deep; this is more than half filled with coffee, finely pounded with a pestle and mortar, and then filled up with water; after being placed for a few seconds on the fire, the contents are poured, or rather shaken, out (being much thicker than chocolate) without the addition of cream or sugar, into a china cup of the size and shape of half an egg-shell, which is enclosed in one of ornamented metal for convenience of holding in the hand.

Later, the Turkish sought to improve the method by adding sugar (a concession to the European sweet tooth) during the boiling process. The improved Turkish recipe is as follows:

First boil the water. For two cups of the beverage add three lumps of sugar and return the boiler to the fire. Add two teaspoonfuls of powdered coffee, stirring well and let the pot boil up four times. Between each boiling the pot is to be removed from the fire and the bottom tapped gently until the froth on the top subsides. After the last boiling pour the coffee first into one cup and then the other, so as to evenly divide the froth.

Egypt and Algeria

Arabic: *qahwah* (coffee berry: *bun*)

In the equatorial provinces of Egypt, many eat the raw berries; or first cook them in boiling water, dry them in the sun, and then eat them. It is a custom to exchange coffee beans in friendly greeting.

Turkish and Arabian coffee customs prevail in Algeria and Egypt, modified to some extent by European contact. The Moorish cafés of Cairo, Tunis, and Algiers have furnished inspiration and copy for writers, artists, and travelers for several centuries. They change little with the years.

In the principal streets and public squares of any town in Algeria, it is a common sight to find a group of people squatting about a portable stove, and a table on which cups are in readiness to receive the boiling coffee. The thirsty traveler approaches the dealer, and for a modest sum he gets his drink and goes on his way; unless he prefers to go inside the café, where he may get several drinks and linger over them, sitting on a mat with his legs crossed and smoking his *chibouque*.

Far East

Cambodian: *kafé*
Chinese: *kia-fey, teoutsé*
Japanese: *kéhi*

European methods are popular in making coffee in China and Japan, and in the French and Dutch colonies. When traveling in the Far East, one of the greatest hardships the coffee lover is called upon to endure is the European bottled coffee extract, which so often supplies chefs with the makings of a most forbidding and lazy cup of coffee.

In Java (Indonesia), a favorite method is to make a strong extract by the French drip process and then to use a spoonful of the extract in a cup of hot milk—a good drink when the extract is freshly made for each service.

COFFEE
IN THE
UNITED STATES

The Introduction of Coffee to North America

Undoubtedly the first to bring knowledge of coffee to North America was Captain John Smith, who founded the colony of Virginia at Jamestown in 1607. Captain Smith became familiar with coffee during his travels in Turkey.

Although the Dutch also had early knowledge of coffee, it does not appear that the Dutch West India Company brought any of it to the first permanent settlement on Manhattan Island in 1624. Nor is there any record of coffee in the cargo of the Mayflower, although it included a wooden mortar and pestle, later used to make "coffee powder."

In the period when New York was New Amsterdam, and under Dutch occupancy, it is possible that coffee may have been imported from Holland, where it was being sold on the Amsterdam market as early as 1640, where regular supplies of the green bean were being received from Mocha; but positive proof is lacking. The Dutch appear to have brought tea across the Atlantic from Holland before coffee.

The English may have introduced the coffee drink into the New York colony. The earliest reference to coffee in America comes in 1668, at which time a beverage made from the roasted beans, and flavored with sugar or honey, and cinnamon, was being drunk in New York.

Coffee first appears in the official records of the New England colony in 1670. In 1683, the year following William Penn's settlement on the Delaware, we find him buying supplies of coffee in the New York market and paying for them at the rate of eighteen shillings and nine pence per pound.

In the pioneer days of the great west, coffee and tea were hard to get; and, instead of them, teas were often made from garden herbs, spicewood, sassafras roots, and other shrubs, taken from the thickets.

How the United States Became a Nation of Coffee Drinkers

Coffee, tea, and chocolate were introduced into North America almost simultaneously in the latter part of the seventeenth century. In the first half of the eighteenth century, tea had made such progress in England, thanks to the propaganda of the British East India Company, that, being moved to extend its use in the colonies, the directors turned their eyes first in the direction of North America. Here, however, King George spoiled their well-laid plans by his unfortunate Stamp Act of 1765, which caused the colonists to raise the cry of "no taxation without representation."

Although the act was repealed in 1766, the right to tax was asserted, and in 1767 was again used, duties being laid on paints, oils, lead, glass, and tea. Once again the colonists resisted; and, by refusing to import any goods of English make, so distressed the English manufacturers that Parliament repealed every tax save that on tea. Despite the growing fondness for the beverage in America, the colonists preferred to get their tea elsewhere as opposed to sacrificing their principles and buying it from England. A brisk trade in smuggling tea from Holland was started.

In a panic at the loss of the most promising of its colonial markets, the British East India Company appealed to Parliament for aid, and was permitted to export tea, a privilege it had never before enjoyed. Cargoes were sent on consignment to selected commissioners in Boston, New York, Philadelphia, and Charleston. The story of the subsequent happenings properly belongs in a book on tea. It is sufficient here to refer to the climax of the agitation against the fateful tea tax, because it is undoubtedly responsible for our becoming a nation of coffee drinkers instead of one of tea drinkers, like England.

The Boston "tea party" of 1773, when citizens of Boston, disguised as Indians, boarded the English ships lying in Boston harbor and threw their tea cargoes into the bay, cast the die for coffee; for there and then originated a subtle prejudice against "the cup that cheers," which 150 years have failed entirely to overcome. Meanwhile, the change wrought in our social customs by this act, and those of like nature following it, in the New York, Pennsylvania, and Charleston colonies, caused coffee to be crowned "king of the American breakfast table" and the sovereign drink of the American people.

Coffee and the Civil War

In General Horace Porter's account *Campaigning with Grant*, we see many references to coffee. Deep in the fiercest snarls of the Wilderness Campaign, we are treated to:

> General Grant, slowly sipping his coffee . . . a full ration of that soothing army beverage . . . The general made rather a singular meal preparatory to so exhausting a day as that which was to follow. He took a cucumber, sliced it, poured some vinegar over it, and partook of nothing else except a cup of strong coffee. The general seemed in excellent spirits, and was even inclined to be jocose. He said to me, "We have just had our coffee, and you will find some left for you." I drank it with the relish of a shipwrecked mariner.

One of the first immediate supplies General Sherman desired from Wilmington, on reaching Fayetteville and lines of communication in March, 1865, was, expressly, coffee. He says so himself, in the second volume of his memoirs. Still more expressly, toward the close of his memoirs, and among final recommendations, the fruit of his experiences in that whole vast war, General Sherman says this for coffee:

> Coffee has become almost indispensable, though many substitutes were found for it, such as Indian corn, roasted, ground and boiled as coffee, the sweet potato, and the seed of the okra plant prepared in the same way. All these were used by the people of the South, who for years could procure no coffee, but I noticed that the women always begged of us real coffee, which seemed to satisfy a natural yearning or craving more powerful than can be accounted for on the theory of habit. Therefore I would always advise that the coffee and sugar ration be carried along, even at the expense of bread, for which there are many substitutes.

Coffee and World War I

The year 1919 awarded coffee one of its brightest honors. An American general said that coffee shared with bread and bacon the distinction of being one of the essentials that helped win the World War for the Allies. So this symbol of human brotherhood has played a not inconspicuous part in "making the world safe for democracy." The new age, ushered in by the Peace of Versailles and the Washington Conference, has for its hand-maidens temperance and self-control. It is to be a world democracy of right living and clear thinking; and among its most precious adjuncts are coffee, tea, and cocoa—because these beverages must always be associated with rational living, with greater comfort, and with better cheer.

Tea and Coffee in the United States

The rise of the United States as a coffee consumer in the last century and a quarter has been marked not only by steadily increased imports as the population of the country increased, but also by a steady growth in per capita consumption, showing that the beverage has been continually advancing in favor with the American people. Today it stands at practically its highest point, each individual man, woman, and child having more than twelve pounds a year, enough for almost 500 cups, allotted to him as his portion. This is four times as much as it was a hundred years ago; and more than twice as much as it was in the years immediately following the Civil War. In general, it is 50 percent more than the average in the twenty years preceding 1897, in which year a new high level of coffee consumption was apparently established, the per capita figure for that year being 10.12 pounds, which has been approximately the average since then.

Coffee and Prohibition

Since the advent of country-wide prohibition in the United States on July 1, 1919, about two pounds more coffee per person, or 80 to 100 more cups, have been consumed than before. Part of this increase is doubtless to be charged to prohibition; but it is yet too early to judge fairly as to the exact effect of "bone-dry" legislation on coffee drinking. The continued growth in the use of coffee in the United States has been in decided contrast to the per capita consumption of tea, which is less now than half a century ago. Another effect of prohibition has been to lead many hotels to feature their coffee service, bringing back the modern type of coffee room.

Since prohibition, the average citizen is drinking 100 more cups of coffee a year than he did in the old days; and a good part of the increase is attributed to newly formed habits of drinking coffee between meals, at soda fountains, in tea and coffee shops, at hotels, and even in the home. In other words, the increase is due to coffee drinking that directly takes the place of malt and spirituous liquors. There have come into being the hotel coffee room; the custom of afternoon coffee drinking; and free coffee service in many factories, stores, and offices.

The Quality of Coffee in the United States

In colonial days, must or ale first gave way to tea, and then to coffee, as a breakfast beverage. Until the Boston Tea Party, coffee was more or less for an after-dinner function, or a between-meals drink, as in Europe. In Washington's time, dinner was usually served at three o'clock in the afternoon, and at informal dinner parties the company "sat till sunset—then coffee."

In no country has there been so marked an improvement in coffee making as in the United States. Although in many places, the national beverage is still indifferently prepared, the progress made in recent years has been so great that the friends of coffee are hopeful that before long it may be said truly that coffee making in America is a national honor and no longer the national disgrace that it was in the past.

Already, in the more progressive homes, and in the best hotels and restaurants, the coffee is uniformly good, and the service all that it should be. The American breakfast cup is a food-beverage because of the additions of milk or cream and sugar; and unlike Europe, this same generous cup serves again as a necessary part of the noonday and evening meals for most people.

The Increase in Coffee Consumption

The question is: Do Mr. Citizen, or Mrs. Citizen, or the little Citizens growing up into the coffee-drinking age, pass his or her or their respective cups along for a second pouring where they used to be satisfied with one? Do they take a cup in the evening as well as in the morning, or do they perhaps have it served to them at an afternoon reception where they used to get something else? In other words, is the coffee habit becoming more intensive as well as more extensive?

There are plenty of very good reasons why it should have become so in the last twenty-five or thirty years; for the improvements in distributing, packing, and preparing coffee have been many and notable. It is a far cry these days from the times when the housewife snatched a couple of minutes amid a hundred other kitchen duties to set a pan over the fire to roast a handful of green coffee beans, and then took two or three more minutes to pound or grind the crudely roasted product into coarse granules for boiling.

For a good many years, the keenest wits of the coffee merchants, not only of the United States but of Europe as well, have been at work to refine the beverage as it comes to the consumer's cup; and their success has been striking. Now the consumer can have his favorite brand not only roasted but packed air-tight to preserve its flavor; and made up, moreover, of growths brought from the four corners of the earth and blended to suit the most exacting taste. He can buy it already ground, or he can have it in the form of a soluble powder; he can even get it with the caffeine element 99 percent removed. It is preserved for his use in paper, tin, or fiber boxes, with wrappings whose attractive designs seem to add something in themselves to the quality. Instead of the old coffee pot, black with long service, he has modern shining percolators and filtration devices; with a new one coming out every little while, to challenge even these. Last but not least, he is being educated to make it properly—tuition free.

It would be surprising, with these and dozens of other refinements, if a far better average cup of coffee were not produced than was served forty years ago, and if the coffee drinker did not show his appreciation by coming back for more.

It will be seen that the gain has been a decided one, fairly steady, but not exactly uniform. In fifty years, John Doe has not quite come to the point where he hands up his cup for a second helping and keeps a meaningful silence. Instead, he stipulates, "Don't fill it quite full; fill it about five-sixths as full as it was before." That is a substantial gain, and one that the next fifty years can hardly be expected to duplicate, in spite of the efforts of our coffee advertisers, our inventors, and our vigorous importers and roasters.

The most striking feature of this fifty-year growth was the big step upward in 1897, when the per capita rose two pounds over the year before and established an average that has been pretty well maintained since. Something of the sort may have taken place again in 1920, when there was a three-pound jump over the year before. It will be interesting to see whether this is merely a jump or a permanent rise; whether our coffee trade has climbed to a hilltop or a plateau.

Coffee Trading

The wholesale coffee buyers in the large importing centers of the United States and Europe recognize two distinct markets in their operations. One of these is called the "spot" market; because the importers, brokers, jobbers, and roasters trading there deal in actual coffee in warehouses in the consuming country. In New York, the spot market is located in the district of lower Wall Street, which includes a block or two each side on Front and Water Streets. Here, coffee importers, coffee roasters, coffee dealers, and coffee brokers conduct their "street" sales.

The other market is designated as the "futures" market; and the trading is not concerned with actual coffee, but with the purchase or sale of contracts for future delivery of coffee that may still be on the trees in the producing country. Futures, or "options" as they are frequently called, are dealt in only on a coffee exchange. The principal exchanges are in New York, Havre, and Hamburg. New Orleans and San Francisco exchange dealers trade on their local boards of trade.

Coffee-exchange contracts are dealt in just like stocks and bonds. They are settled by the payment of the difference, or "margin;" and the option of delivering actual coffee is seldom exercised. Generally, the operations are either in the nature of ordinary speculation on margin or for the legitimate purpose of effecting "hedges" against holdings or short sales of actual coffees.

The New York Coffee and Sugar Exchange—the most important in the world, because of the volume of its business—deals in all coffees from North, South, and Central America, the West Indies, and the East Indies (except those of the Robusta variety).

In the coffee trade, there are three kinds of brokers —floor, spot, and cost and freight.

Floor brokers are those who buy and sell options on the Coffee Exchange for a fixed consideration.

Spot brokers are those who deal in actual coffee, selling from jobber to jobber, or representing out-of-town houses; the seller paying a commission of about fifteen cents a bag in small lots, and half of 1 percent in large lots.

Cost and freight brokers represent Brazilian accounts, and generally receive a brokerage of 1¼ percent. On out-of-town business, they usually split the commission with the out-of-town or "local" brokers. The out-of-town brokers sometimes, however, deal directly with the importer. All brokers except floor brokers are sometimes called "street brokers." Most of the large New York, New Orleans, and San Francisco brokerage houses also do a commission business, handling one or more Brazilian or other coffee-producing country accounts.

///

Coffee and the Law

The United States have no coffee law as they have a tea law—prescribing "purity, quality and fitness for consumption"—but buyers and sellers of green coffees are required to observe certain well-defined federal rules and regulations relating specifically to coffee.

Up to the year 1906, when the Pure Food and Drugs Act became law, the green coffee trade was practically unhampered; and several irregularities developed, calling into existence federal laws that were designed to protect the consumer against trade abuses, and at the same time to raise the standards of coffee trading.

Under these regulations, it is illegal to import into this country a coffee that grades below a No. 8 Exchange type, which generally contains a large proportion of sour or damaged beans, known in the trade as "black jack," or damaged coffee, as found in "skimmings." *Black jack* is a term applied to coffee that has turned black during the process of curing, or in the hold of a ship during transportation; or it may be due to a blighting disease.

Another ruling is intended to prevent the sale of artificially "sweated" coffee, which has been submitted to a steaming process to give the beans the extra-brown appearance of high grade East Indian and Mocha coffees which have been naturally "sweated" in the holds of sailing vessels during the long journey to American ports. Up to the time that the Pure Food and Drugs Act went into effect, artificial "sweating" was resorted to by some coffee firms; and out of that practice grew a suit that resulted in a federal court decision sustaining the Pure Food Act, and classifying the practice as adulteration and misbranding.

The Act also is intended to prevent the sale of coffees under trade names that do not properly belong to them. For example, only coffees grown on the island of Java can properly be labeled and sold as Javas; coffees from Sumatra, Timor, etc., must be sold under their respective names. Likewise the name Mocha may be used only for coffees of Arabia. Before the Pure Food law was enacted, it was frequently the custom to mix Bourbon Santos with Mocha and to sell the blend as Mocha. Also, Abyssinian coffees were generally known in the trade as Longberry Mocha, or just straight Mocha; and Sumatra growths were practically always sold as Javas. Traders used the names of Mocha and Java because of the high value placed upon these coffees by consumers, who, before Brazil dominated the market, had practically no other names for coffee.

One of the most celebrated coffee cases under the Pure Food Act was tried in Chicago, February, 1912. The question was, whether in view of the long-standing trade custom, it was still proper to call an Abyssinian coffee (Longberry Mocha), Mocha. The defendant was charged with misbranding, because he sold as Java and Mocha a coffee containing Abyssinian coffee. The court decided that the product should be called Abyssinian Mocha. But since then, it has become generally accepted that only coffee grown in the province of Yemen in Arabia could properly be known as Mocha coffee.

Another important ruling, concerning coffee buyers and sellers, prohibits the importation of green coffees coated with lead chromate, Prussian blue, and other substances, to give the beans a more stylish appearance than they have normally. Such "polished" coffees find great favor in the European markets, but are now denied admittance here.

For years a practice persisted of re-bagging certain Central American growths in New York. In this way Bucaramangas frequently were transformed into

Bogotas, Rios became Santos, Bahias and Victorias were sold as Rios, and the misbranding of peaberry was quite common. A celebrated case grew out of an attempt by a New York coffee importer and broker to continue one of these practices after the Pure Food Act made it a criminal offense. The defendants, who were found guilty of conspiracy, and who were fined $3,000 each, mixed, re-packed, and sold under the name P.A.L. Bogota, a well-known Colombian mark, eighty-four bags of washed Caracas coffee.

The practice in Holland of grading Santos coffees—by selecting beans most like Java beans, and polishing and coloring them to add verisimilitude—known as "manipulated Java," became such a nuisance in 1912 that United States consuls refused to certify invoices to the United States unless accompanied by a declaration that the produce was "pure Java, neither mixed with other kinds nor counterfeited."

The United States Bureau of Chemistry ruled in February of 1921, that *Coffea robusta* could not be sold as Java coffee, or under any form of labeling which tended, either directly or indirectly, to create the impression that it was *Coffea arabica*, so long and favorably known as Java coffee. This was in line with the Department of Agriculture's previous definition that coffee was the seed of the *Coffea arabica* or *Coffea liberica*, and that Java coffee was *Coffea arabica* from Java. *Coffea robusta* was barred from deliveries on the New York Coffee Exchange in 1912.

During the greater part of the year 1918, the United States government assumed virtually full control of coffee trading. It was a wartime measure, and was intended to prevent speculation in coffee contracts and freight rates, to cut down the number of vessels carrying coffee so as to provide more ships for transporting food and soldiers to Europe, and to put the coffee merchants on rations during the stress of war. On February 4, 1918, importers and dealers were placed under license; and two days later, rules were issued through the Food Administration fixing the maximum price for coffee for the spot month in the "futures" markets at eight and a half cents, prohibiting dealers from taking more than normal prewar profits, or holding supplies in excess of ninety days' requirements, and greatly limiting resales. On May 8, the United States Shipping Board fixed the "official" freight rate from Rio de Janeiro to New York at $1.50 per bag, which, without control, had risen to as high as $4 and more, as compared with the ordinary rate of thirty-five cents before the war. On January 12, 1919, two months after the armistice was signed, the rules were withdrawn, and the coffee trade was left to carry on its business under its own direction.

America's Coffee Legacy

Lovers of coffee in the United States are in a better position to obtain an ideal cup of the beverage than those in any other country. While imports of green coffee are not so carefully guarded as tea imports, there is a large measure of government inspection designed to protect the consumer against impurities, and the Department of Agriculture is zealous in applying the pure food laws to insure against misbranding and substitution. The department has defined coffee as "a beverage resulting from a water infusion of roasted coffee and nothing else."

Today no reputable merchant would think of selling even loose coffee for other than what it is. And the consumer can feel that, in the case of packaged coffee, the label tells the truth about the contents.

COFFEE
AS AN
ART FORM

Keats on Coffee

In John Keats's amusing fantasy, *Cap and Bells*, the Emperor Elfinan greets Hum, the great soothsayer, and offers him refreshment:

> *"You may have sherry in silver, hock in gold, or glass'd*
> *champagne*
> *. . . what cup will you drain?"*
> *"Commander of the Faithful!" answered Hum,*
> *"In preference to these, I'll merely taste*
> *A thimble-full of old Jamaica rum."*
> *"A simple boon," said Elfinan; "thou mayst*
> *Have Nantz, with which my morning coffee's laced."*

But Hum accepts the glass of Nantz, without the coffee, "made racy with the third part of the least drop of crème de citron, crystal clear."

Coffee Sonnet
by Francis Saltus

One of the most delightful coffee poems in English is Francis Saltus's nineteenth-century sonnet on "the voluptuous berry," as found in *Flasks and Flagons*:

Coffee

Voluptuous berry! Where may mortals find
Nectars divine that can with thee compare,
When, having dined, we sip thy essence rare,
And feel toward wit and repartee inclined?

Thou wert of sneering, cynical Voltaire,
The only friend; thy power urged Balzac's mind
To glorious effort; surely Heaven designed
Thy devotees superior joys to share.

Whene'er I breathe thy fumes, 'mid Summer stars,
The Orient's splendent pomps my vision greet.
Damascus, with its myriad minarets, gleams!
I see thee, smoking, in immense bazaars,
Or yet, in dim seraglios, at the feet
Of blond Sultanas, pale with amorous dreams!

Coffee Poetry
by Arthur Gray

Arthur Gray, in *Over the Black Coffee* (1902), has made the following contribution to the poetry of coffee, with an unfortunate reflection on tea, which might well have been omitted:

Coffee

O, boiling, bubbling, berry, bean!
Thou consort of the kitchen queen—
Browned and ground of every feature,
The only aromatic creature,
For which we long, for which we feel,
The breath of morn, the perfumed meal.

For what is tea? It can but mean,
Merely the mildest go-between.
Insipid sobriety of thought and mind
It "cuts no figure"—we can find—
Save peaceful essays, gentle walks,
Purring cats, old ladies' talks—

But coffee! can other tales unfold.
Its history's written round and bold—
Brave buccaneers upon the "Spanish Main,"

The army's march across the length'ning plain,
The lone prospector wandering o'er the hill,
The hunter's camp, thy fragrance all distill.

So here's a health to coffee! Coffee hot!
A morning toast! Bring on another pot.

The First Appearance of Coffee on the Stage

Coffee was first "dramatized," so to speak, in England in 1667, where Charles II and the Duke of York attended the first performance of *Tarugo's Wiles*, or the *Coffee House*, a comedy by Thomas St. Serf. Samuel Pepys described the drama as "the most ridiculous and insipid play I ever saw in my life."

The piece opens in a lively manner, with a request on the part of its fashionable hero for a change of clothes. Accordingly, Tarugo puts off his "vest, hat, perriwig, and sword," and serves the guests to coffee, while the apprentice acts his part as a gentleman customer. Presently other "customers of all trades and professions" come dropping into the coffee house. These are not always polite to the supposed coffee-man; one complains of his coffee being "nothing but warm water boyl'd with burnt beans," while another desires him to bring "chocolette that's prepar'd with water, for I hate that which is encouraged with eggs." The pedantry and nonsense uttered by a "schollar" character is, perhaps, an unfair specimen of coffee-house talk; it is especially to be noticed that none of the guests ventures upon the dangerous ground of politics.

In the end, the coffee-master grows tired of his clownish visitors, saying plainly, "This rudeness becomes a suburb tavern rather than my coffee house," and with the assistance of his servants he "thrusts 'em all out of doors, after the schollars and customers pay."

The Coffee Cantata

The most notable contribution to the "music of coffee," if one may be permitted the expression, is the Coffee Cantata of Johann Sebastian Bach, the German organist and the most modern composer of the first half of the eighteenth century. He hymned the religious sentiment of protestant Germany. In his Coffee Cantata, he tells in music the protest of the fair sex against the libels of the enemies of the beverage, who at the time were actively urging in Germany that it should be forbidden women, because its use made for sterility!

Bach's Coffee Cantata is No. 211 of the Secular Cantatas, and was published in Leipzig in 1732. In German it is known as *Schweigt stille, plaudert nicht* (Be silent, do not talk). It is written for soprano, tenor, and bass solos and orchestra. Bach used as his text a poem by Piccander. The cantata is really a sort of one-act operetta—a jocose production representing the efforts of a stern parent to check his daughter's propensities in coffee drinking, the new-fashioned habit. One seldom thinks of Bach as a humorist; but the music here is written in a mock-heroic vein, the recitatives and arias having a merry flavor, hinting at what the master might have done in light opera.

The libretto shows the father Schlendrian, or Slowpoke, trying by various threats to dissuade his daughter from further indulgence in the new vice, and, in the end, succeeding by threatening to deprive her of a husband. But his victory is only temporary. When the mother and the grandmother indulge in coffee, asks the final trio, who can blame the daughter?

Bach uses the spelling coffee—not kaffee. The cantata was sung as recently as December 18, 1921, at a concert in New York by the Society of the Friends of Music, directed by Arthur Bodanzky.

Lieschen, or Betty, the daughter, has a delightful aria, beginning, "Ah, how sweet coffee tastes—lovelier than a thousand kisses, sweeter far than muscatel wine!"

Sculpture and Coffee

Research has discovered only one piece of sculpture associated with coffee—the statue of the Austrian hero Kolschitzky, the patron saint of the Vienna coffee houses. It graces the second-floor corner of a house in the Favoriten Strasse, where it was erected in his honor by the Coffee Makers's Guild of Vienna. The great "brother-heart" is shown in the attitude of pouring coffee into cups on a tray from an oriental service pot.

//

Coffee and the Art of Divination

An early English magazine (1731) contains an account of divination by coffee grounds. The writer pays an unexpected visit, and "surprised the lady and her company in close cabal over their coffee. The interest was very intent upon one whom, by her address and intelligence, he guessed was a tire woman, to which she added the secret of divining by coffee grounds. She was then in full inspiration, and with much solemnity observing the atoms around the cup; on the one hand sat a widow, on the other a maiden lady. They assured me that every cast of the cup is a picture of all one's life to come, and every transaction and circumstance is delineated with the exactest certainty."

The advertisement used by this seer is quite interesting:

An advise is hereby given that there has lately arrived in this city (Dublin) the famous Mrs. Cherry, the only gentlewoman truly learned in the occult science of tossing of coffee grounds; who has with uninterrupted success for some time past practiced to the general satisfaction of her female visitants. Her hours are after prayers are done at St. Peter's Church, until dinner.

(N.B. She never requires more than 1 oz. of coffee from a single gentlewoman, and so proportioned for a second or third person, but not to exceed that number at any one time.)

If the one ounce of coffee represented her payment for reading the future, the charge could not be considered exorbitant!

The Most Beautiful Coffee House in the World

This is the Caffè Pedrocchi in Padua, Italy. Erected by the poor lemonade vendor and coffee seller, Antonio Pedrocchi.

The celebrated Caffè Pedrocchi, the center of life in the city of Padua, Italy, in the early part of the nineteenth century, is one of the most beautiful buildings erected in Italy. Its use is apparent at first glance. It was begun in 1816, opened June 9, 1831, and completed in 1842. Antonio Pedrocchi (1776–1852), an obscure Paduan coffee-house keeper, tormented by a desire for glory, conceived the idea of building the most beautiful coffee house in the world, and carried it out.

THE
PROPERTIES
OF
COFFEE

Types of Coffee in the United States

More than a hundred different kinds of coffee are bought and sold in the United States. All of them belong to the same botanical genus, and practically all to the same species, the *Coffea arabica*; but each has distinguishing characteristics which determine its commercial value in the eyes of the importers, roasters, and distributors.

The American trade deals almost exclusively in *Coffea arabica*, although in the latter years of the World War, increasing quantities of *robusta* and *liberica* growths were imported, largely because of the scarcity of Brazilian stocks and the improvement in the preparation methods.

All coffees used in the United States are divided into two general groups, Brazils and Milds. Brazils comprise those coffees grown in São Paulo, Minãs Gerais, Rio de Janeiro, Bahia, Victoria, and other Brazilian states. The Milds include all coffees grown elsewhere. In 1921 Brazils made up about three-fourths of the world's total consumption. They are regarded by American traders as the "price" coffees, while Milds are considered as the "quality" grades.

Brazil coffees are classified into four great groups, which bear the names of the ports through which they are exported: Santos, Rio, Victoria, and Bahia. Santos coffee is grown principally in the state of São Paulo; Rio, in the state of Rio de Janeiro and the state of Minãs Gerais; Victoria, in the state of Espirito Santo; and Bahia, in the state of Bahia. All of these groups are further subdivided according to their bean characteristics and the districts in which they are produced.

//

The Characteristics of Brazils

Santos coffees, considered as a whole, have the distinction of being the best grown in Brazil. Rios rank next, Victorias coming third in favor, and Bahias fourth. Of the Santos growths, the best that is known in the trade is Bourbon, produced by trees grown from Mocha seed brought originally from the French island colony of Bourbon (now Réunion) in the Indian Ocean. The true Bourbon is obtained from the first few crops of Mocha seed. After the third or fourth year of bearing, the fruit gradually changes in form, yielding in the sixth year the flat-shaped beans which are sold under the trade name of Flat Bean Santos. By that time, the coffee has lost most of its Bourbon characteristics. The true Bourbon of the first and second crops is a small bean, and resembles the Mocha, but makes a much handsomer roast with fewer "quakers." The Bourbons grown in the Campinas district often have a red center.

///

The Characteristics of Milds

Among the Mild coffees, there is a much greater variation in characteristics than is found among the Brazilian growths. This is due to the differences in climate, altitude, and soil, as well as in the cultural, processing, storage, and transportation methods employed in the widely separated countries in which Milds are produced.

Mild coffees generally have more body, more acidity, and a much finer aroma than Brazils. From the standpoint of quality, they are far more desirable in the cup. As a rule they have also better appearance, or "style," both in the green and in the roast, due to the fact that greater care is exercised in picking and preparing the higher grades. Milds are important for blending purposes, most of them possessing distinctive individual characteristics, which increase their value as blending coffees.

Aging Coffee

Although it has long been held that green coffee improves with age, and there is little doubt that this is true in so far as roasting merits are concerned; the question has been raised among coffee experts as to whether age improves the drinking qualities of all coffees alike.

Rio coffees should improve with age, as they are naturally strong and earthy. Age might be expected to soften and to mellow them and others having like characteristics. If, however, the coffee is mild in cup quality in the first instance, then it may be asked if age does not weaken it so that in time it must become quite insipid. Several years ago, a New York coffee expert pointed out that this was what happened to Santos coffees. The new crop, he said, was always a more pleasant and enjoyable drink than the old crop, because it was a more pronounced mild coffee in the cup.

Determining the Quality of the Coffee Bean

The coffee bean is graded by the number of imperfections contained in it. These imperfections are black beans, broken beans, shells, immature beans ("quakers"), stones, and pods. For counting the imperfections, the black bean has been taken as the basis unit, and all imperfections, no matter what they may be, are calculated in terms of black beans, according to a scale, which is practically as follows:

Black-Bean Scale

THE NUMBER AND TYPE OF IMPERFECTION	THE EQUIVALENT UNITS OF BLACK BEANS
3 shells	1 black bean
5 "quakers"	1 black bean
5 broken beans	1 black bean
1 pod	1 black bean
1 medium-sized stone	1 black bean
2 small stones	1 black bean
1 large stone	2–3 black beans

Renovating Damaged Coffees

Often, charlatans have resorted to sophisticated methods in order to ostensibly "improve" damaged or cheap coffee. The glazing, coloring, and polishing of the green beans was openly and covertly practiced until restricted by law. The steps employed did not actually improve the coffee by any means, but merely put it into condition for more ready sale.

An apparently sincere endeavor to renovate damaged coffee was made by Feedeeick Evans when he treated it with an aqueous solution of sulfuric acid having a density of 10.5° Baumé. After agitation in this solution, the beans were washed free from acid and dried. In this manner, discolorations and impurities were removed and the beans given a fuller appearance.

The addition of glucose, sucrose, lactose, or dextrin to green coffees is practiced by some, with the objective of giving a mild taste and strong aroma to "hard" coffees. The addition is accomplished by impregnating, with or without the aid of vacuum, the beans with a moderately concentrated solution of the sugar, the liquid being of insufficient quantity to effect extraction. When the solution has completely disseminated through the kernels, they are removed and dried. Upon subsequent roasting, a decided amelioration of flavor is secured.

Another method developed by Gebrüder von Niessen comprises the softening of the outer layers of the beans by steam, cold or warm water, or brine, and then surrounding them with an absorbent paste or powder, such as china clay, to which a neutralizing agent such as magnesium oxide may be added. After drying, the clay can be removed by brushing or by causing the beans to travel between oppositely reciprocated wet cloths. In the development of this process, von Niessen evidently argued that the so-called "caffetannic acid" is the "harmful" substance in coffee, and that it is concentrated in the outer layers of the coffee beans. If these were his precepts, the question of their correctness and of the efficiency of his process becomes a moot one.

A procedure which aims at cleaning and refining raw coffee, and which has been the subject of much polemical discussion, is that of Julius Thum's. It entails the placing of the green beans in a perforated drum; just covering them with water, or a solution of sodium chloride or sodium carbonate, at 65° to 70°C; and subjecting them to a vigorous brushing for 1 to 5 minutes, according to the grade of coffee being treated. The value of this method is somewhat doubtful, as it would not seem to accomplish any more than simple washing. In fact, if anything, the process is undesirable; as some of the extractive matters present in the coffee, particularly caffeine, will be lost. The experimental data for this procedure is also questionable, and so this method does not carry much weight.

Taste-Testing Coffee

Before the beginning of the twentieth century, practically all the coffees bought and sold in the United States were judged for merit simply by the appearance of the green or roasted bean. Since that time, the importance of testing the drinking qualities has become generally recognized; and today every progressive coffee buyer has his sample roasting and testing outfit with which to carry out painstaking cup tests. Both buyers and sellers use the cup test, the former to determine the merits of the coffee he is buying, and the latter to ascertain the proper value of the crop under consideration. Frequently a test is made to fix the relative desirability of various growths considered as a whole, using composite samples that are supposed to give representation to an entire crop.

The first step in testing coffee is to compare the appearance of the green bean of a crop with a sample of known standard value for that particular kind of coffee. The next step is to compare the appearance when roasted. Then comes the appearance and aroma test, when it is ground; and finally, the most difficult of all, the trial of the flavor and aroma of the liquid.

Naturally the tester gives much care to proper roasting of the samples to be examined. He recognizes several different kinds of roasts which he terms the light, the medium, the dark, the Italian, and the French roasts, all of which vary in the shadings of color, and each of which gives a different taste in the cup. The careful tester watches the roast closely to see whether the beans acquire a dull or bright finish, and to note also if there are many "quakers," or off-color beans. When the proper roasting point is reached, he smells the beans while still hot to determine their aroma. In some growths and grades, he will frequently smell of them as they cool off, because the character changes as the heat leaves them, as in the case of many Maracaibo grades.

After roasting, the actual cup-testing begins. Two methods are employed: the blind cup test, in which there is no clue to the identity of the kind of coffee in the cup; and the open test, in which the tester knows beforehand the particular coffee he is to examine. The former is most generally employed by buyers and sellers; although a large number of experts, who do not let their knowledge interfere with their judgment, use the open method.

In both systems the amount of ground coffee placed in the cup is carefully weighed so that the strength will be standard. Generally, the cups are marked on the bottom for identification after the examination. Before pouring on the hot water to make the brew, the aroma of the freshly ground coffee is carefully noted to see if it is up to standard. In pouring the water, care is exercised to keep the temperature constant in the cups, so that the strength in all will be equal. When the water is poured directly on the grounds, a crust or scum is formed. Before this crust breaks, the tester sniffs the aroma given off; this is called the wet-smell, or crust, test, and is considered of great importance.

Of course, the taste of the brew is the most important test. Equal amounts of coffee are sipped from each cup, the tester holding each sip in his mouth only long enough to get the full strength of the flavor. He spits out the coffee into a large brass cuspidor which is designed for the purpose. The expert never swallows the liquor.

Cup-testing calls for keenly developed senses of sight, smell, and taste, and the faculty for remembering delicate shadings in each sense. By sight, the coffee man judges the size, shape, and color of the green and roasted bean, which are important factors in determining commercial values. He can tell also whether the coffee is of the washed or unwashed variety, and whether it contains many imperfections such as quakers, pods, stones, brokens, off-colored beans, and the like. By his sense of smell of the roast and of the brew, he gauges the strength of the aroma, which also enters into the valuation calculation. His palate tells him many things about a coffee brew—if the drink has body and is smooth, rich, acidy, or mellow; if it is winy, neutral, or harsh; if it is musty, groundy, woody, or grassy; or if it is rank, sour, muddy, or bitter. These are trade designations of the different shades of flavor to be found in the various coffees coming to the North American market; and each has an influence on the price at which they will be sold.

On Coffee Substitutes

Trading upon the credulity of the hypochondriac and the caffeine-sensitive, in recent years there has appeared in America and abroad a curious collection of so-called coffee substitutes. They are "neither fish nor flesh, nor good red herring." Most of them have been shown by official government analyses to be sadly deficient in food value—their only alleged virtue. One of our contemporary attackers of the national beverage bewails the fact that no palatable hot drink has been found to take the place of coffee. The reason is not hard to find. There can be no substitute for coffee. Dr. Harvey W. Wiley has ably summed up the matter by saying, "A substitute should be able to perform the functions of its principal. A substitute to a war must be able to fight. A bounty-jumper is not a substitute."

Buying Coffee

With a hundred different kinds of coffee coming to this market from nineteen countries, so many combinations are possible that there is sure to be a straight coffee or a blend to suit any taste. And those who may have been frightened into the belief that coffee is not for them should do a little experimenting before exposing themselves to the dangers of the coffee-substitute habit.

If you are accustomed to buying loose coffee, have your dealer do a little experimental blending for you until you find a coffee to suit your palate. Some expert blends are to be found among the leading packaged brands. But you really cannot do better than to trust your case to a first-class grocer of known reputation. He will guide you right if he knows his business; and if he doesn't, then he doesn't know his business—try elsewhere. Test him out along this line:

Let us reason together, Mr. Grocer. Let us consider these facts about coffee: green coffee improves with age? Granted. As soon as it is roasted, it begins to lose in flavor and aroma? Certainly. Grinding hastens the deterioration? Of course. Therefore, it is better to buy a small quantity of freshly roasted coffee in the bean and grind it at the time of purchase or at home just before using? Absolutely!

If your grocer reacts in this fashion, he need only supply you with a quality coffee at fair price and you need only to make it properly to obtain the utmost of coffee satisfaction.

Coffee Blends

Once upon a time, it was thought that Java and Mocha were the only worthwhile blends, but now we know that a Bogota coffee from Colombia and a Bourbon Santos from Brazil make a most satisfying drink. And if the individual seeker should happen to be a caffeine-sensitive, there are coffees so low in caffeine content, like some Puerto Ricans, as to overcome this objection; while there are other coffees from which the caffeine has been removed by a special treatment.

Some connoisseurs still cling to the good old two-thirds Java and one-third Mocha blend, but the author has for years found great pleasure in a blend composed of half Medellin Bogota, one-quarter Mandheling "Java," and one-quarter Mocha. However, this blend might not appeal to another's taste, and the component parts are not always easy to get.

Another pleasing blend is composed of Bogota, washed Maracaibo, and Santos, equal parts.

If you are epicurean, you will want to try the fancy Mexicans, Cobáns, Sumatra growths, Meridas, and some from the "Kona side" of Hawaii.

COFFEE MAKING AND DRINKING

Preparing the Perfect Cup

In preparing the perfect cup of coffee, then, the coffee must be of good grade, and freshly roasted. It should, if possible, be ground just before using. The author has found a fine grind, about the consistency of fine granulated sugar, the most satisfactory. For general home use, a device that employs filter paper or filter cloth is best; for the epicure an improved porcelain French percolator (drip pot) or an improved cloth filter will yield the utmost of coffee's delights. Drink it black, sweetened or unsweetened, with or without cream or hot milk, as your fancy dictates.

It should be remembered that to make good coffee no special pot or device is necessary. Good coffee can be made with any china vessel and a piece of muslin. But to make it in perfection, pains must be taken with every step in the process, from roaster to cup.

Methods and Materials

Today, people of all classes in the United States begin and end the day with coffee. In the home, it is prepared by boiling, infusion or steeping, percolation, and filtration; in the hotels and restaurants, by infusion, percolation, and filtration. The best practice favors true percolation (French drip), or filtration.

Steeping coffee in American homes is usually performed in a china or earthenware jug. The ground coffee has boiling water poured upon it until the jug is half full. The infusion is stirred briskly. Next, the jug is filled by pouring in the remainder of the boiling water; the infusion is again stirred, then permitted to settle, and finally is poured through a strainer or filter cloth before serving.

When a pumping percolator or a double glass filtration device is used, the water may be cold or boiling at the beginning as the maker prefers. Some wet the coffee with cold water before starting the brewing process.

For genuine percolator, or drip coffee, French and Austrian china drip pots are mostly employed.

On Boiling Ground Coffee

The old-time boiling method of making coffee has gone out of style, because the average consumer is becoming aware of the fact that it does not give a drink of maximum efficiency. Boiling the ground coffee with water results in a large loss of aromatic principles by steam distillation, a partial hydrolysis of insoluble portions of the grounds, and a subsequent extraction of the products thus formed, which give a bitter flavor to the beverage. Also, the maintenance of a high temperature by the direct application of heat has a deleterious effect upon the substances in solution. This is also true in the case of the pumping percolator, and any other device wherein the solution is caused to pass directly into steam at the point where heat is applied. Warm and cold water extract about the same amount of material from coffee; but with different rates of speed, an increase in temperature decreasing the time necessary to effect the desired result.

Boiled coffee is usually cloudy, due to the suspension of fine particles resulting from the disintegration of the grounds by the violence of boiling. The usual procedure in clarifying the decoction is to add the white of an egg or some eggshells, the albumen of which is coagulated upon the fine particles by the heat of the solution, and the particles thus weighted sink to the bottom. Even this procedure, requiring much attention, does not give as clear a solution as some of the other extraction procedures employed. The conditions to which coffee is subjected during boiling are the worst possible, as both grounds and solution undergo hydrolysis, oxidation, and local overheating, while the caffeol is steam-distilled from the brew. Many persons who have long been accustomed to drinking the relatively bitter beverage thus produced are not satisfied by coffee made in any other way; but this is purely a perversion of taste, for none of the properties are present which make coffee so prized by the epicure.

On Steeping Coffee

Steeping, in which cold water is added to the coffee and the mixture brought up to a boil, does not subject the coffee to so strenuous conditions as boiling. Local overheating and hydrolysis occur, but not to so great an extent as in boiling; and most of the effects of oxidation and volatilization of caffeol are absent. However, extraction is rather incomplete, due to lack of thorough admixture of the water and coffee.

When coffee is to be made under the best conditions, the temperature of the water used and of the extract after it is made should not fluctuate. In the pumping percolator, as in the steeping method, the temperature varies greatly from the time the extraction is started to the completion of the operation. This is deleterious. Also, local overheating of the infusion occurs at the point of application of the heat; and because of the manner in which the water is brought into contact with the coffee, the degree of extraction shows inefficiency. Spraying of the water over the coffee never permits the grounds to be completely covered with water at any one time, and the opportunity offered for channeling is excessive. The principle of thorough extraction demands that, as the substance being extracted becomes progressively more exhausted, fresh solvent should be brought into contact with it. In the pumping percolator, the solution pumped over the grounds becomes more concentrated as the grounds become exhausted; so that the time taken to reach the degree of extraction desired is longer, and an appreciable amount of relatively concentrated liquor is retained by the grounds.

On Brewing Coffee

The simplest procedure to follow is that in which boiling water is poured over ground coffee suspended on a filtering medium in such a manner that the extracting water will slowly pass through the coffee and be received in a containing vessel, which obviates further contact of the beverage with the grounds. The water as it comes into contact with the ground coffee extracts the soluble material, and the solution is removed by gravity. Fresh water takes its place; so that, if the filter medium be of the proper fineness, the water flows through at the correct rate of speed, and complete extraction is effected with the production of a clear solution. Thus a maximum extraction of desirable materials is obtained in a short time with a minimum of hydrolysis, oxidation, and loss of caffeol; and if the infusion be consumed at once, or kept warm in a contrivance embodying the double-boiler principle, the effects of local overheating are avoided. Also, with the use of an appropriate filter, a finer grind of coffee can be used than in the other devices, without obtaining a turbid brew. All this works toward the production of a desirable drink.

The Coffeemaker

There are several devices on the market, some using a paper filter, and some cloth, which operate on the brewing principal and give very good coffee. The use of paper presents the advantage of using a new and clean filter for each brew, whereas the cloth must be carefully kept immersed in water between brews to prevent its fouling.

Contrivances operating on the filtration principle have been designed for use on a large scale in conjunction with coffee urns, and have proven quite successful in causing all of the water to go slowly through the coffee without channeling, thus accomplishing practically complete extraction. The majority of urns are still operated with bags, of which the ones with sides of heavier material than the bottom obtain the most satisfactory results, as the majority of the water must pass through the coffee instead of out through the sides of the bag. Greatest efficiency, when bags are used, is obtained by repouring until all of the liquid has passed twice through the coffee; further repouring extracts too much of the astringent hydrolysis products. The bags, when not in use, should not be allowed to dry but should be kept in a jar of cold water. The urns provided with water jackets keep the brew at almost a constant temperature and avoid the deterioration incident to temperature fluctuation.

The coffee liquor acts on metals in such a manner as to lower the quality of the drink, so that metals of any sort, and by all means irons, should be avoided as far as possible. Instead, earthenware or glass, preferably a good grade of the former, should be employed as far as possible in the construction of coffee-making devices.

Of the various metals, silver, aluminum, Monel metal, and tin (in the order named) are least attacked by coffee infusions; and besides these, nickel, copper, and well-enameled iron (absolutely free from pin holes) may be used without much danger of contamination. Rings for coffee-urn bags should be made of tinned copper, Monel metal, or aluminum. Even if coffee be made in metal contrivances, the receptacles in which it stands should be made of earthenware or of glass.

Painstaking care should be given to the preservation of the coffeemakers in a state of cleanliness, as upon this depends the value of the brew. Dirt, fine grounds, and fat (which will turn rancid quickly) should not be allowed to collect on the sides, bottom, or in angles of the device difficult of access. Nor should any source of metallic or exterior contamination be allowed to remain on the apparatus.

The Correct Way to Make Coffee

1. Buy a good grade of freshly roasted coffee from a responsible dealer.

2. Grind it very fine, and at home, just before using.

3. Allow a rounded tablespoonful for each beverage cup.

4. Make it in a French drip pot or in some filtration device where freshly boiling water is poured through the grind but once. A piece of muslin and any china receptacle make an economical filter.

5. Avoid pumping percolators, or any device for heating water and forcing it repeatedly through the grounds. Never boil coffee.

6. Keep the beverage hot and serve it "black" with sugar and hot milk, or cream, or both.

Coffee at the Waldorf

The method of preparing coffee for individual service in the Waldorf-Astoria, New York, which has been adopted by many first-class hotels and restaurants that do not serve urn-made coffee exclusively, is the French drip plus careful attention to all the contributing factors for making coffee in perfection, and is thus described by the hotel's steward:

A French china drip coffee pot is used. It is kept in a warm heater; and when the coffee is ordered, this pot is scalded with hot water. A level tablespoonful of coffee, ground to about the consistency of granulated sugar, is put into the upper and percolator part of the coffee pot. Fresh boiling water is then poured through the coffee and allowed to percolate into the lower part of the pot. The secret of success, according to our experience, lies in having the coffee freshly ground, and the water as near the boiling point as possible, all during the process. For this reason, the coffee pot should be placed on a gas stove or range. The quantity of coffee can be varied to suit individual taste. We use about ten percent more ground coffee for after dinner cups than we do for breakfast. Our coffee is a mixture of Old Government Java and Bogota.

The New Orleans Method of Brewing

The Creole, or French market, coffee for which New Orleans has long been famous is made from a concentrated coffee extract prepared in a drip pot. First, the ground coffee has poured over it sufficient boiling water thoroughly to dampen it, after which further additions of boiling water, a tablespoonful at a time, are poured upon it at five-minute intervals. The resulting extract is kept in a tightly corked bottle for making *café au lait* or *café noir* as required. A variant of the Creole method is to brown three tablespoonfuls of sugar in a pan, to add a cup of water, and to allow it to simmer until the sugar is dissolved; to pour this liquid over ground coffee in a drip pot; to add boiling water as required; and to serve black or with cream or hot milk, as desired.

In New Orleans, coffee is often served at the bedside upon waking, as a kind of early breakfast function.

Appealing to All Senses

There is something more to coffee than its caffeine stimulus and its action on the taste buds of the tongue and mouth. The sense of smell and the sense of sight play important roles. To get all the joy there is in a cup of coffee, it must look good and smell good, before one can pronounce its taste good. It must woo us through the nostrils with the wonderful aroma that constitutes much of the lure of coffee.

And that is why, in the preparation of the beverage, the greatest possible care should be observed to preserve the aroma until the moment of its psychological release. This can only be done by having it appear at the same instant that the delicate flavor is extracted—roasting and grinding the bean much in advance of the actual making of the beverage will defeat this objective. Boiling the extraction will perfume the house; but the lost fragrance will never return to the dead liquid called coffee, when served from the pot whence it was permitted to escape.

The Role of Sugar in Coffee

The important and indispensable part that sugar plays in the makeup of the American cup of coffee was ably set forth by Fred Mason, vice president of the American Sugar Refining Co., when he said:

The coffee cup and the sugar bowl are inseparable table companions. Most of us did not realize this until the war came, with its attendant restrictions on everything we did, and we found that the sugar bowl had disappeared from all public eating places. No longer could we make an unlimited number of trips to the sugar bowl to sweeten our coffee; but we had to be content with what was doled out to us with scrupulous care—a quantity so small at times that it gave only a hint of sweetness to our national beverage.

Then it was that we really appreciated how indispensable the proper amount of sugar was to a good, savory cup of coffee, and we missed it as much as we would seasoning from certain cooked foods. Secretly we consoled ourselves with the promise that if the day ever came when sugar bowls made their appearance once more, filled temptingly with the sweet granules that were "gone but not forgotten," we should put an extra lump or an additional spoonful of sugar into our coffee to help us forget the joyless war days.

Since sugar is so necessary to our enjoyment of this popular beverage, it is obvious that a considerable part of all the sugar we consume must find its way into the national coffee cup. The stupendous amount of 40 billion cups of coffee is consumed in this country each year. Taking two teaspoonfuls or two lumps as a fair average per cup, we find that about 800,000,000 pounds of sugar, almost one-tenth of our total annual consumption, are required to sweeten Uncle Sam's coffee cup. This is specially significant when one considers that, with the single exception of Australia, the United States consumes more sugar per capita than any country on Earth.

Sugar adds high food value to the stimulative virtues of coffee. The beverage itself stimulates the mental and physical powers, while the sugar it contains is fuel for the body and furnishes it with energy. Sugar is such a concentrated food that the amount used by the average person in two cups of coffee is enough to furnish the system with more energy than could be derived from forty oysters on the half-shell.

Culinary Coffee

When Mrs. Ida C. Bailey Allen prepared a booklet of recipes for the Joint Coffee Trade Publicity Committee, she introduced them with the following remarks on the use of coffee as a flavoring agent:

Although coffee is our national beverage, comparatively few cooks realize its possibilities as a flavoring agent. Coffee combines deliciously with a great variety of food dishes and is especially adapted to desserts, sauces and sweets. Thus used it appeals particularly to men and to all who like a full-bodied pronounced flavor.

For flavoring purposes coffee should be prepared just as carefully as when it is intended for a beverage. The best results are obtained by using freshly made coffee, but when, for reasons of economy, it is desirable to utilize a surplus remaining from the mealtime brew, care should be taken not to let it stand on the grounds and become bitter.

When introducing made coffee into a recipe calling for other liquid, decrease this liquid in proportion to the amount of coffee that has been added. When using it in a cake or in cookies, instead of milk, a tablespoonful less to the cup should be allowed, as coffee does not have the same thickening properties.

In some cases, better results are gained if the coffee is introduced into the dish by scalding or cooking the right proportion of ground coffee with the liquid which is to form the base. By this means the full coffee flavor is obtained, yet the richness of the finished product is not impaired by the introduction of water, as would be the case were the infused coffee used. This method is advisable especially for various desserts which have milk as a foundation, as those of the custard variety and certain types of Bavarian Creams, Ice Cream, and the like. The right proportion of ground coffee, which is generally a tablespoonful to the cup, should be combined with the cold milk or cream in the double-boiler top and should then be scalded over hot water, when the mixture should be put through a very fine strainer or cheese cloth, to remove all grounds.

Coffee can be used as a flavoring in almost any dessert or confection where a flavoring agent is employed.

On Cool Coffee Beverages

The *mazagran*—sweetened cold coffee to which water or ice has been added—originated in Algeria. It probably took its name from the fortress of the same name reserved to France by the Treaty of Tafna in 1837. It is said that the French colonial troops were first served with a drink made from coffee syrup and cold water on marches near *Mazagran*, formerly spelled *Masagran*. Upon their return to the French capital, they introduced the idea, with the added fillip of service in tall glasses, in their favorite cafés, where it became known as *café mazagran*. Variants are coffee syrup with seltzer, and with hot water. "This fashion of serving coffee in glasses," says Jardin, "has no *raison d'être*, and nothing can justify abandoning the cup for coffee."

On iced coffee and the use of coffee in summer beverages in general, Mrs. Ida C. Bailey Allen writes as follows:

Iced Coffee. This is not only a delicious summer drink, but it also furnishes a mild stimulation that is particularly grateful on a wilting hot day. It may be combined with fruit juices and other ingredients in a variety of cooling beverages which are less sugary and cloying than the average warm weather drink and for that reason it is generally popular with men.

Coffee that is to be served cold should be made somewhat stronger than usual. Brew it according to your favorite method and chill before adding sugar and cream. If cracked ice is added make sure the coffee is strong enough to compensate for the resulting dilution. Mixing the ingredients in a shaker produces a smoother beverage topped with an appetizing foam.

It is a convenience, however, to have on hand a concentrated syrup from which any kind of coffee-flavored drink may be concocted on short notice and without the necessity of lighting the stove. Coffee left over from meals may be used for the same purpose, but it should be kept in a covered glass or china dish and not allowed to stand too long. A coffee syrup made after the following recipe will keep indefinitely.

Coffee Syrup

INGREDIENTS
2 quarts of very strong coffee
3½ pounds sugar

1. The coffee should be very strong, as the syrup will be largely diluted. The proportion of a pound of coffee to 1¾ quarts of water will be found satisfactory.

2. This may be made by any favorite method, cleared and strained, then combined with the sugar, brought to boiling point, and boiled for two or three minutes.

3. It should be canned while boiling, in sterilized bottles. Fill them to overflowing and seal as for grape juice or for any other canned beverage.

THE
PHARMACOLOGY
OF
COFFEE

NOTE: Portions of the chapter on The Pharmacology of Coffee have been prepared under the author's direction by Charles W. Trigg, industrial fellow of the Mellon Institute of Industrial Research.

The Supposed Miraculous Properties of Coffee

One cannot fail to note, in connection with the introduction of coffee into England, that the beverage suffered most from the indiscretions of its friends. On the one hand, the quacks of the medical profession sought to claim it for their own. On the other, more or less ignorant laymen attributed to the drink such virtues as its real champions among the physicians never dreamed of. It was the favorite pastime of its friends to exaggerate coffee's merits; and of its enemies, to vilify its users. All this furnished good "copy" for and against the coffee house, which became the central figure in each new controversy.

From the early English author who damned it by calling it "more wholesome than toothsome," to Pasqua Rosée and his contemporaries, who urged its more fantastic claims, it was forced to make its way through a veritable morass of misunderstanding and intolerance. No harmless drink in history has suffered more at the hands of friend and foe.

While its friends hail it as a panacea, its enemies retorted that it was a slow poison. In France and in England there were those who contended that it produced melancholy, and those who argued it was a cure for the same. Dr. Thomas Willis (1621–1673), a distinguished Oxford physician said he would sometimes send his patients to the coffee house rather than to the apothecary's shop.

As a cure for drunkenness its "magic" power was acclaimed by its friends, and grudgingly admitted by its foes. Coffee was praised by one writer as a deodorizer. Another, in his treatise concerning its use with regard to the plague, said if its qualities had been fully known in 1665, "learned men of that time would have recommended it." As a matter of fact, in Gideon Harvey's *Advice Against the Plague*, published in 1665, we find, "coffee is commended against the contagion."

//

Coffee and Insomnia

Insomnia is a condition frequently attributed to coffee, but that the authorities disagree on this ground is shown by Dr. Harvey Wiley's contention, "We know beyond doubt that the caffeine (in coffee) makes a direct attack on the nerves and causes insomnia."

While Woods Hutchinson observes:

> Oddly enough, a cup of hot, weak tea or coffee, with plenty of cream and sugar, will often help you to sleep, for the grateful warmth and stimulus to the lining of the stomach, drawing the blood into it and

away from the head, will produce more soothing effects than the small amount of caffeine will produce stimulating and wakeful ones. ☕

The writer has often had people remark to him that while black coffee sometimes kept them awake, coffee with cream or sugar or both made them drowsy.

//

Coffee Drinking and Longevity

It is known that the habitual coffee drinker generally enjoys good health, and some of the longest-lived people have used it from their earliest youth without any apparent injury to their health. Nearly every one has an acquaintance who has lived to a ripe old age despite the use of coffee. Quoting Metchnikoff from his work *The Prolongation of Life*:

In some cases centenarians have been much addicted to the drinking of coffee. The reader will recall Voltaire's reply when his doctor described the grave harm that comes from the abuse of coffee, which acts as a real poison. "Well," said Voltaire, "I have been poisoning myself for nearly eighty years." There are centenarians who have lived longer than Voltaire and have drunk still more coffee. Elizabeth Durieux, a native of Savoy, reached the age of 114. Her principal food was coffee, of which she took daily as many as forty small cups. She was jovial and a boon table companion, and used black coffee in quantities that would have surprised an Arab. Her coffee-pot was always on the fire, like the tea-pot in an English cottage.

The entire matter resolves itself into one of individual tolerance, resistivity, and constitution. Numerous examples of young abstainers who have died and coffee drinkers who have still lived on can be found, and vice versa, the preponderance of instances being in neither direction. Bodies of persons killed by accident have been painstakingly examined for physiological changes attributable to coffee; but no difference between those of coffee and of non-coffee drinkers (ascertained by careful investigation of their life history) could be discerned. In the long run, it is safe to say that the effect of coffee drinking upon the prolongation or shortening of life is neutral.

Coffee and Digestion

In general, a moderate amount of coffee stimulates appetite, improves digestion, and relieves the sense of plenitude in the stomach. It increases intestinal peristalsis, acts as a mild laxative, and slightly stimulates secretion of bile. Excessive use, however, profoundly disturbs digestive function, and promotes constipation and hemorrhoids.

There is much evidence to support the view that "neither tea, coffee, nor chicory in dilute solutions has any deleterious action on the digestive ferments, although in strong solutions such an action may be manifest." After conducting exhaustive experiments with various types of coffee, Dr. Julius Lehmann concluded that ordinary coffee is without effect on the digestion of the majority of sound persons, and may be used with impunity.

When coffee passes directly to the stomach, its sole immediate action is to dilute the previous contents, just as other ingested liquids do. Eventually the caffeine content is absorbed by the system, and from then on stimulation is apparent.

The statement has sometimes been made that milk or cream causes the coffee liquid to become coagulated when it comes into contact with the acids of the stomach. This is true, but does not carry with it the inference that indigestibility accompanies this coagulation. Milk and cream, upon reaching the stomach, are coagulated by the gastric juice; but the casein product formed is not indigestible. These liquids, when added to coffee, are partially acted upon by the small acid content of the brew, so that the gastric juice action is not so pronounced, for the coagulation was started before ingestion, and the coagulable constituent, casein, is more dilute in the cup as consumed than it is in milk. Accordingly, the particles formed by it in the stomach will be relatively smaller and more quickly and easily digested than milk per se. It has been observed that coffee containing milk or cream is not as stimulating as black coffee. The writer believes that this is probably due to mechanical inclusion of caffeine in the casein and fat particles, and also to some adsorption of the alkaloid by them. This would materially retard the absorption of the caffeine by the body, spread the action over a longer period of time, and hence decrease the maximum stimulation attained.

A Careful Account of the Coffee Headache

From the *British Homeopathic Review*:

If the quantity of coffee taken be immoderately great and the body be very excitable and quite unused to coffee, there occurs a semilateral headache from the upper part of the parietal bone to the base of the brain. The cerebral membranes of this side also seem to be painfully sensitive, the hands and feet becoming cold, and sweat appears on the brows and palms. The disposition becomes irritable and intolerant, anxiety, trembling and restlessness are apparent. . . . I have met with headaches of this type which yielded readily to coffee and with many more in which the indicated remedy failed to act until the use of coffee as a beverage was abandoned. The eyes and ears suffer alike from the super-excitation of coffee. There is a characteristic toothache associated with coffee.

The Coffee Addiction Myth

"**H**abit-forming" is one of the adjectives often used in describing coffee, but it is a fact that coffee is much less likely than alcoholic liquors to cause ill effects. A man rarely becomes a slave of coffee, and excessive drinking of this beverage never produces a state of moral irresponsibility or leads to the commission of crime. Dr. J. W. Mallet, in testimony given before a federal court, stated that caffeine and coffee were not habit-forming in the correct sense of the term. His definition of the expression is that the habit formed must be a detrimental and injurious one—one which becomes so firmly fixed upon a person forming it that it is thrown off with great difficulty and with considerable suffering, continuous exercise of the habit increasing the demand for the habit-forming drug. It is well known that the desire ceases in a very short period of time after cessation of use of caffeine-containing beverages, so that in that sense, coffee is not habit-forming.

It has been shown that the daily administration of coffee produces a certain degree of tolerance, and that the doses must be increased to obtain toxic results. The doctor and astronomer William Harkness has been quoted as stating that "taken in moderation, coffee is one of the most wholesome beverages known. It assists digestion, exhilarates the spirits, and counteracts the tendency to sleep."

Effects of Coffee on Children

Dr. Jonathan Hutchinson makes the following weighty pronouncement:

> In reference to my suggestion to give children tea and coffee. I may explain that it is done advisedly. There is probably no objection to their use even at early ages. They arouse the dull, calm the excitable, prevent headaches, and fit the brain for work. They preserve the teeth, keep them tight in their place, strengthen the vocal chords, and prevent sore throat. To stigmatize these invaluable articles of diet as "nerve stimulants" is an erroneous expression, for they undoubtedly have a right to rank as nerve nutrients.

In a study of the effects of coffee drinking upon 464 school children, C. K. Taylor found a slight difference in mental ability and behavior, unfavorable to coffee. About 29 percent of these children drank no coffee; 46 percent drank a cup a day; 12 percent, 2 cups; 8 percent, 3 cups; and the remainder, 4 or more cups a day. The measurements of height, weight, and hand strength also showed a slight advantage in favor of the non-coffee drinkers. If these results be taken as truly representative, their indication is obvious. However, it seems desirable to repeat these experiments upon other groups; at the same time noting carefully the factors of environment, and other diet, before any criterion is made.

As a refutation to this experimental evidence is the practical experience of the inhabitants of the Island of Groix, off the Brittany coast, whose annual consumption of coffee is nearly 30 pounds per capita, being ingested both as the roasted bean and as an infusion. It is reported that many of the children are nourished almost entirely on coffee soup up to ten years of age, yet the mentality and physique of the populace does not fall below that of others of the same stock and educational opportunities.

It is a difficult matter definitely to set an age below which coffee should not be drunk, as the time of reaching maturity varies with climate and ancestral origin. Yet, from a theoretical standpoint, children before or during the adolescent period should be limited to the use of a rather small amount of tea and coffee as beverages, as their poise and nerve control have not reached a stage of development sufficient to warrant the stimulation incident to the consumption of an appreciable quantity of caffeine.

COFFEE,
A
DIVINE
THESAURUS

Encomiums and descriptive phrases applied to the plant, the berry, and the beverage.

The Plant

The precious plant
This friendly plant
Mocha's happy tree
The gift of Heaven
The plant with the jessamine-like flowers
The most exquisite perfume of Araby the Blest
Given to the human race by the gift of the gods

The Berry

The magic bean
The divine fruit
Fragrant berries
Rich, royal berry
Voluptuous berry
The precious berry
The healthful bean
The Heavenly berry
The marvelous berry
This all-healing berry
Yemen's fragrant berry
The little aromatic berry
Little brown Arabian berry

Thought-inspiring bean of
  Arabia
The smoking, ardent beans
  Aleppo sends
That wild fruit which gives
  so beloved a drink

The Beverage

Nepenthe
Festive cup
Juice divine
Nectar divine
Ruddy mocha
A man's drink
Lovable liquor
Delicious mocha
The magic drink
This rich cordial
Its stream divine
The family drink
The festive drink
Coffee is our gold
Nectar of all men
The golden mocha
This sweet nectar
Celestial ambrosia
The friendly drink
The cheerful drink
The essential drink
The sweet draught
The divine draught
The grateful liquor
The universal drink
The American drink
The amber beverage
The convivial drink
The universal thrill
King of all perfumes
The cup of happiness

The soothing draught
Ambrosia of the gods
The intellectual drink
The aromatic draught
The salutary beverage
The good-fellow drink
The drink of democracy
The drink ever glorious
Wakeful and civil drink
The beverage of sobriety
A psychological necessity
The fighting man's drink
Loved and favored drink
The symbol of hospitality
This rare Arabian cordial
Inspirer of men of letters
The revolutionary beverage
Triumphant stream of
sable
Grave and wholesome
liquor
The drink of the
intellectuals
A restorative of sparkling
wit
Its color is the seal of its
purity
The sober and wholesome
drink
Lovelier than a thousand
kisses

This honest and cheering
beverage

A wine which no sorrow
can resist

The symbol of human
brotherhood

At once a pleasure and a
medicine

The beverage of the
friends of God

The fire which consumes
our griefs

Gentle panacea of
domestic troubles

The autocrat of the
breakfast table

The beverage of the
children of God

King of the American
breakfast table

Soothes you softly out of
dull sobriety

Coffee, which makes the
politician wise

Its aroma is the pleasantest
in all nature

The indispensable beverage
of strong nations

The stream in which we
wash away our sorrows

The enchanting perfume
that a zephyr has brought

Favored liquid which fills
all my soul with delight

The delicious libation we
pour on the altar of
friendship

This invigorating drink
which drives sad care
from the heart

INDEX